Person Centred Planning in a Learning Disability Service

Jenny Pearce

Supporting the Learning Disability Awards Framework

Higher Professional Diploma in Learning Disability Services (Level 4)

Unit 2: Person Centred Planning in a Learning Disability Service

British Library Cataloguing in Publication Data

A CIP record for this book is available from the Public Library

© BILD Publications 2006

BILD Publications is the imprint of:
British Institute of Learning Disabilities
Campion House
Green Street
Kidderminster
Worcestershire DY10 IJL

Telephone: 01562 723010
Fax: 01562 723029
E-mail: enquiries@bild.org.uk

Website: www.bild.org.uk

ISBN 1 904082 99 8

BILD publications are distributed by:
BookSource
50 Cambuslang Road
Cambuslang
Glasgow G32 8NB

Telephone: 0845 370 0067
Fax: 0845 370 0064

For a publications catalogue with details of all BILD books and journals telephone 01562 723010, e-mail enquiries@bild.org.uk or visit the BILD website: www.bild.org.uk

Printed in the UK by Latimer Trend & Company Ltd, Plymouth

About the British Institute of Learning Disabilities

The British Institute of Learning Disabilities is committed to improving the quality of life for people with a learning disability by involving them and their families in all aspects of our work, working with government and public bodies to achieve full citizenship, undertaking beneficial research and development projects and helping service providers to develop and share good practice.

Acknowledgements

A number of individuals, families and professionals have helped me to put together this workbook, and I am very grateful for their contributions.
In particular I wish to thank:

David Cooper

Members of Leicester City Learning Disability Partnership Board,
Person Centred Planning Working Group

Jonathan Gittings, Gaynor Earle, Bob Furr and Maria Richardson at Applegarth

Gill and Michael Huddlestone

Annie Lawton and friends

Lesley Barcham and the staff at BILD

About the author

Jenny Pearce has worked in social care for over 30 years, working mainly with people with learning disabilities in a variety of settings. She is a qualified social worker and has a Masters Degree in Learning Disability Studies from the University of Birmingham. She currently works for a voluntary sector organisation in the East Midlands and is the lead for person centred planning for a Learning Disability Partnership Board. Jenny also works as a freelance trainer and consultant, is an Associate Lecturer for the Open University and has published training resources on learning disabilities.

Contents

		Page
	Introduction	9
Chapter 1	The principles of person centred planning	13
Chapter 2	Person centred planning styles	31
Chapter 3	Skills and approaches	47
Chapter 4	Barriers and challenges	63
Chapter 5	Funding and resources	75
Chapter 6	The impact of person centred planning	85
Chapter 7	The wider context of person centred planning	89
	References	97
	Resources	99

Introduction

This book is intended for managers and senior practitioners concerned with support services for people with learning disabilities who want to continue their professional development. It should also be of interest to senior staff and managers who are preparing for the Learning Disability Awards Framework (LDAF) Higher Professional Diploma in Learning Disability Services (Level 4) Unit 2 Person Centred Planning in a Learning Disability Service and studying S/NVQ at Level 4.

The purpose of this book is to:

- explore the principles, implementation and impact of person centred planning

- investigate ways of maximising the effectiveness of person centred planning for individuals

- review her/his own practice within the person centred planning process

- analyse the wider context in which person centred planning operates, including resources, constraints and opportunities

How the book is organised

The book has seven chapters:

Chapter 1   *The principles of person centred planning* considers the principles, key features and origins of person centred planning and how it contrasts with other approaches to care planning. It also reviews the legislative and policy context in the United Kingdom.

Chapter 2   *Person centred planning styles* looks at the different styles and techniques that have been developed and what makes each one special.

Chapter 3   *Skills and approaches* focuses on the range of roles that can be involved in person centred planning, the skills needed and the importance of record keeping.

Chapter 4   *Barriers and challenges* is about approaches that enable people to be in control of their own lives.

Chapter 5   *Resources* considers the ways that funding is allocated on both a local and a national level, how allocation impacts upon availability of the whole range of resources and how shortfalls can be highlighted, to stimulate change.

Chapter 6   *The impact of person centred planning* is primarily reflective to enable managers to learn from implementing person centred planning and to respond proactively to the impact that person centred planning has on individual lives.

Chapter 7   *The wider context of person centred planning* draws together the strands of the whole book, putting person centred planning into the wider context of services, both locally and nationally.

Following chapter 7 there are references and a resources section that includes useful contact addresses and suggestions for additional reading.

The LDAF Higher Professional Diploma (Level 4)

The Higher Professional Diploma is intended for senior workers in roles associated with services supporting adults with learning disabilities, eg supported employment or supported living, residential or respite services, day care and community based support services. There are two pathways to the diploma, *Managing Learning Disability Services* and *Senior Practitioner in Learning Disability Services*, each requiring a particular combination of units from the unit bank. Learners need to complete 12 units to achieve the full qualification. Further information is available at www.ldaf.org.uk

Person Centred Planning in a Learning Disability Service, the unit addressed in this book, is a mandatory unit for both pathways. All of the topics required for successful completion of this unit are covered in this book. The aims and outcomes of this LDAF unit are listed below.

Aims

This unit aims to enable the learner to:

- explore the principles, implementation and impact of person centred planning

- investigate ways of maximising the effectiveness of person centred planning for individuals

- review her/his own practice within the person centred planning process

- analyse the wider context in which person centred planning operates, including resources, constraints and opportunities

Outcomes

On successful completion of this unit the learner will be able to:

- apply the principles of person centred planning

- evaluate the impact of person centred planning

- understand how the service user is empowered to lead their own person centred planning process

- recognise the skills and approaches needed to contribute to person centred planning

- analyse the barriers and challenges that may be faced in implementing operson centred planning

- understand systems for the allocation and distribution of resources to meet the needs of people with a learning disability

- discuss the wider context within which person centred planning takes place

Non-diploma readers

For readers not undertaking the LDAF diploma, the book serves as a stand-alone text, which contributes to Continuing Professional Development (CPD) or a qualification other than LDAF.

Activities and reflections

Learning is only as good as the use we put it to – in this instance, its impact upon practice. There are likely to be topics in this book with which you are already very familiar. A particular slant might cause you to think about these in different ways. There will be other areas less familiar to you. To capitalise on opportunities for interaction with the text there are, at intervals throughout the book, activities, comments and key points which encourage you to consider how the particular issue under discussion relates to your own situation and experience. This structure is also designed to help you to develop your evidence for assessment if you are a LDAF candidate. Completion of all the activities will give you all the evidence needed for your portfolio of evidence, to successfully complete this unit. In addition, you might find them useful as the basis for discussion at staff meetings or for staff supervision purposes.

Chapter 1

The principles of person centred planning

Introduction

Person centred planning has become a key concept in services for people with learning disabilities today. You may, in the course of your work, have come across different planning styles and processes over the years. As a result, some people may be tempted to ask whether person centred planning isn't 'just the latest way of doing individual programme plans or assessments?' (Sanderson et al, 1997).

In this chapter you will be helped to focus on:

- the principles and key features of person centred planning

- the history and origins of person centred planning

- the differences between person centred planning and other approaches to care planning

- how person centred planning is promoted by current legislation, government policies and guidelines

- where you can obtain help and guidance

The principles and key features of person centred planning

Helen Sanderson tells us that person centred planning 'is not just a collection of new planning styles' (Sanderson et al, 1997). So what is it? It is:

- a way of helping people who want to make some changes in their lives

- an empowering approach to helping people plan their future and organise the supports and services they need

- a set of beliefs and values, not just another model of support

These beliefs and values are crucial to true person centred planning, and can be stated as:

- All members of society have the same rights. People with learning disabilities have the same rights and are entitled to the same opportunities and choices as everyone else. In other words, *all means all.*

- *Independence means choice and control.* The 'readiness' model (in which people are assessed and only allowed to move on towards more independence when they have enough skills) is replaced by the 'support' model which just asks 'what support do you need to do what you want to do?' In this way, support ceases to be a negative thing, but is seen as something that everyone needs, with some needing more than others.

- If people with learning disabilities are to be supported to have choice and control, others must be prepared to give away power. This *power sharing* is essential, and has the potential to totally change the way services are designed and delivered, or whether the person even uses services at all.

- *Inclusive communities* enable a challenge to discrimination, social exclusion and oppression. This concept of inclusion means more than people with learning disabilities living where everyone else lives and using the same facilities. It is about people actually being accepted as citizens and being involved, along with other members of the community, in what is going on. Segregation does not enable people with learning disabilities to be part of their local communities and so prevents the development of healthy communities based on diversity, inclusion and respect. This means that people with learning disabilities should be supported to develop and maintain relationships, which are the vital key to inclusion, and to be involved in networks of friends and families.

- Person centred planning is based on *shared action*, in which people who know and care about the person are committed to enabling the process of change.

ACTIVITY 1: **The 'readiness' model and the need for people to be valued**

Imagine that you are a clerical assistant in a large computer software company. You would like to apply for promotion to office manager over a team of six other clerical staff. Your clerical skills are good and, although you have not managed people before, you reckon you have good people skills and you are ready to learn.

You get an interview, but there you are asked lots of difficult questions, such as:

- Why are you applying for the job when you have never managed people?

- How can the company improve its sales profits next year?

- What new objectives should the company set, why, and how will it achieve them?

You are told you would need a masters degree in management for the job, and it does not look as though you have the right knowledge and skills. You are told that you are not skilled enough for the job, but you can reapply when you think that you are able to meet the criteria.

Think about this experience and list all your immediate thoughts to the following questions.

- How would you feel during the interview?

- How might you react towards your interviewers?

- How would you feel after the interview?

- What course of action might you decide upon?

Comment

I know that if this had been me I might have cried. I would certainly have felt humiliated and stupid, dried up completely or reacted in a defensive or aggressive way towards the interviewers. Afterwards, I would have felt devalued; I would have lost a lot of my confidence and might never apply for promotion again. Alternatively, I might try so hard that I actually would succeed, but it would turn me into a very aggressive, competitive person.

Are there parallels here with the situation of many people with learning disabilities? Very often, people are set targets for achievement and told that once they can gain certain skills and succeed in certain ways, then and only then will they be ready for independent living (or ready to get a job, or get married, or whatever it is they are striving for). This is known as the 'readiness' model. Hopefully, this exercise can make us feel uncomfortable about the experience that many people with learning disabilities are forced to go through as we measure them against our own criteria for 'success'.

Jo and Peter

Jo and Peter met through the day centre that they both attended and developed a close and loving relationship. They wanted to get married and dreamed of having their own home. However, staff told them that they needed to learn about keeping a house, shopping, cooking and lots of other things before they were ready for marriage. They were told that they would be helped to gain the skills they needed but nothing actually changed. Eventually, Jo's parents decided to move to another part of the country, taking her with them. No one offered to help Jo keep in contact with Peter through telephone calls or letters and Peter did not know Jo's address. He never saw her again.

Key points

Person centred planning is based on some basic beliefs and values:

- **All means all**

- **Independence means choice and control**

- **Power sharing**

- **Inclusive communities**

- **Shared action**

The implementation of these beliefs and values results in ways of planning that differ significantly from traditional models:

- The person with a learning disability is at the centre of the process.

- Family members and friends are full partners, resulting in interdependence.

- Person centred planning focuses on what the person can do and what support they need. It does not focus on disability and failure. The person, rather than the professionals, is acknowledged as the expert.

- There is a shared commitment to action and change. This means that services may have to change, and the focus moves from better services to inclusive communities.

- Person centred planning does not finish when the plan is written. It begins here, and requires continuous listening, learning and action as the person develops and opportunities unfold.

Key points

There are five key features to person centred planning:

- **The person is at the centre of the process.**

- **Family members and friends are full partners.**

- **The focus is on ability, what is important to the person and the supports needed.**

- **There is a shared commitment to action and change.**

- **When the plan is finished, the process is only just beginning.**

The history and origins of person centred planning

You may be surprised to realise that the roots of person centred planning go right back to the 1960s. A useful account of the journey from those early days until the early 1990s is given by Connie Lyle O'Brien and John O'Brien in their paper 'The Origins of Person-Centred Planning: a community of practice perspective' published in 2000 by Responsive Systems Associates Inc. This article, which can be accessed from the Paradigm website at www.paradigm-uk.org is an intensive read for managers but really explains how person centred planning developed from a number of different starting points. (There is also a fact sheet about person centred planning and useful links available from the BILD website at www.bild.org.uk) The writers talk about a 'community of practice', which is a term that is taking on increasing relevance in Britain today. Communities of practice are defined as 'groups of people informally bound together by shared expertise and a passion for a joint enterprise' (Wenger and Snyder, 2000 in Lyle, O'Brien and O'Brien, 2000) and the early days in North America involved a number of different people approaching the issues of institutionalisation and devalued lifestyles in different ways.

The key concepts explored in this article are the shared passion that enabled the person centred planning to develop, the way ideas crossed the Atlantic in both directions and the 'community of practice' that enabled the principles of normalisation to grow and evolve into person centred planning. It explains the different approaches employed but also the need to remain focused on the person and not be rooted in one particular model.

I shall now look at some of the key approaches, theories and cultural issues that have contributed to the concept of person centred planning. These are:

- normalisation and social role valorisation

- ordinary life principles

- O'Brien's five service accomplishments

- the social model of disability and the disability rights movement

- care in the community and institutional closure

- social inclusion

- individual programme planning

- good practice in social work assessment

- Valuing People

Normalisation and social role valorisation

'Normalisation theory' was first put forward in North America in 1969 by Wolf Wolfensberger in his work *The Origin and Nature of our Institutional Models*. However, the concept goes back a good ten years earlier to Scandinavia. Essentially, Wolfensberger suggests that there are lifestyles, such as family life, work and relationships, which are valued in society as normal. People with learning disabilities have the same rights to these norms as anyone else, but they can only be achieved through full integration within society. Sadly, many people misinterpreted 'normalisation' as being 'same' which, if you think about it, would result in a very boring society to live in. Wolfensberger went on to refine his theory with the concept of 'social role valorisation'. This now seems to be appalling jargon, and Wolfensberger was certainly no disciple of plain English. The idea was that there are roles within society which are valued (for instance being a parent, having a paid job) and it is everyone's right to play such roles, rather than devalued roles such as 'client' or 'inmate'. O'Brien and Tyne in 1981 defined social role valorisation as 'the use of means which are valued in our society to develop and support characteristics and behaviour which are likewise valued'.

Looking back, some of the thinking seems somewhat confused: in a series of training videos called *Bringing People Back Home*, produced by the Tizard Centre at the University of Kent, people are portrayed learning how to vacuum clean and dust their home, although the roles of 'cleaner' or 'housewife' are actually quite devalued in our society. That is not to say people should not be helped to look after their own home, but as a sideline rather than the main activity, unless they love doing it. Otherwise life could be very dull.

During the 1970s and early 1980s a system of analysing services to see whether they could support the principles of normalisation was developed. PASS (Program Analysis of Service Systems) and its successor PASSING (Program Analysis of Service Implementation of Normalisation Goals) helped people to realise the problems with trying to support individualised lifestyles in services. PASS was the first tool that had been developed to enable a critical review of services from the perspective of the person using them and as such challenged services about their existing practice. Often there was found to be a wide gap or disconnect between the stated aims of the service and what people with learning disabilities experienced in practice. PASS and PASSING helped the realisation to emerge that it would take more than an ordinary house in an ordinary street to fulfil the principles of normalisation, but that a total change was needed in the way people were supported and the control that people had over their lives.

Ordinary life principles

In Britain, the principles of normalisation were developed further by the work of the King's Fund Centre. *An Ordinary Life* published in 1980, stated that 'Our goal is to see mentally handicapped people in the mainstream of life, living in ordinary houses, in ordinary streets, with the same range of choices as any citizen, and mixing as equals with the other, and mostly not handicapped, members of their own community' ('mental handicap' being the accepted terminology at the time).

Ordinary life principles were stated as:

- People with learning disabilities have the same human value as anyone else, and the same human rights.

- Living like others within the community is both a right and a need.

- Services must recognise the individuality of people with learning disabilities.

Remember that this was some time before the Human Rights Act became law in Britain and so was quite radical thinking for the time.

O'Brien's five essential accomplishments

John O'Brien's name has already been mentioned because of the impact of his work on learning disability services. He applied the principles of normalisation and social role valorisation to service design to try to offer a framework for achieving valued life styles. He called this the 'Five Essential Accomplishments':

Community presence: the experience of taking part in community life and living and spending leisure time with other members of the community

Choice: the experience of making choices in both small, everyday matters and large, life-defining matters (including where to live and with whom to live)

Competence: the experience of gaining new skills and participating in meaningful activities with whatever assistance is required

Respect: the experience of having a valued place among a network of people and valued roles in community life (not being treated as a second-class citizen)

Community participation: the experience of being part of a growing network of valued relationships which includes close friends, people who are not disabled or paid professionals

Each accomplishment is closely linked to the other four through mutual interdependence.

Figure 1: O'Brien's five essential accomplishments

Figure 1 demonstrates the central position played by community participation, which has since been developed more fully into the concept of community inclusion. In other words, it is not sufficient to just take part in the community; the community needs to fully include and embrace people with learning disabilities.

Yet again, the five accomplishments have often lost much of their meaning in translation. A key misinterpretation is the assumption that 'community' means 'the places where people go' (the pub, the shops, the church) whereas it actually means the people themselves. Thus, it is no use being in the pub if you are not mixing with the other people there, as you continue to be isolated. Many 'group living' models involve people with learning disabilities going in a group of service users and staff to the day centre, to the shops, to the pub, etc in a minibus or specialised transport and actually having no more contact with anybody else than they had in the institutions – or even less.

The social model of disability and the disability rights movement

The care of people with learning disabilities up until the 1960s was deeply rooted in the 'medical model' which saw the 'handicapped' person as the problem and focused on disease and cure. People were incarcerated in hospitals, the very nature of which assumes that people are ill and the workers are there to cure them. The 'social model', on the other hand, recognises that people are disabled by society's attitudes towards them. It focuses upon the person, not the impairment, and asks what is needed to support the person to take their full role in society. Thus, the social model sees that the problem arises from the person living within a disabling society, rather than the person themselves being the problem.

These two opposing models can be clearly demonstrated by Figure 2.

Figure 2: Medical model and social model

	Problem	Response
Medical model	Person with a learning disability	Institutionalisation, segregation Person devalued and dehumanised
Social model	Society's attitudes to person with a learning disability	Individualised services Person gains control

While all the challenging concepts of human rights, the need for inclusive communities and 'ordinary' lifestyles took hold, the disability rights movement gained momentum both in America and Britain. A major campaigner in the 1970s was the Campaign for People with Mental Handicap (CMH) which was later renamed Values into Action (VIA) and which still has a strong voice today. VIA is a small but influential organisation that has been at the forefront of the campaign for social inclusion for many years. It is primarily a campaigning organisation, working to eradicate discrimination and to promote citizenship for people with learning disabilities (see their website at www.viauk.org). Self-advocacy organisations began to gain strength, and for the first time the voice of people with learning disabilities began to be heard.

Care in the community and institutional closure

In recent years some enlightening work has been done by writers such as Dorothy Atkinson and Jan Walmsley, helping people with learning disabilities to tell the story of their own life within the institutions. These 'oral histories' are very powerful in bringing home to us the injustices and devalued experiences of people like Mabel Cooper whose life story is told in *Forgotten Lives* by Atkinson et al (1997). Irving Goffman, in his book *Asylums* (1961), wrote about the concept of the 'total institution' in which people were treated as a homogenous group rather than as individuals, and where there were two separate worlds for staff and inmates, with staff wielding power. People living in the institutions lost all their former identity and simply became 'inmates', and over time the inmates took on an acceptance of their powerlessness and loss of self as they became totally institutionalised.

The move for change came slowly, despite a groundswell from the 1970s onwards following several major scandals. The problems with institutions were, however, well catalogued, and are summarised below.

Problems with institutions

Size: Life revolves around the group, not the individual.

Segregation: People with learning disabilities are separated from non-disabled people with separate facilities so they cannot take part in society.

Location: Services are located in isolated, rural settings or away from residential areas without accessible shops or local facilities and without easy access to public transport.

Routines: People's lives are dominated by inflexible routines rather than the environment adapting to suit the needs or wants of individuals.

Attitudes: People with learning disabilities are thought of as 'mad' or 'bad' and a threat to society.

Privacy: Personal activities are monitored and relationships are observed, discussed and interfered with. Personal possessions are at risk and privacy and personal space are hard to find and protect.

Choice: Personal choice is limited or non-existent. Choices are made by other people, activities take place in groups which have been decided by other people. There is little or no control over major life decisions and fewer opportunities to make everyday life choices.

Dependence and powerlessness: People are encouraged by the institution to expect decisions to be made for them, so they become dependent and learn how to be helpless, losing the ability to choose or make decisions. This then fulfils the expectations of others that they cannot take responsibility for themselves.

Social networks: People only meet and mix with other service users, staff and professionals who are paid to be there. Any relationship that forms may be vetoed if seen as unsuitable. Friendships from the past may be lost, families become distant and there are few opportunities to meet anyone outside the institution. Sexuality is negated and denied.

The first piece of legislation to make community care a government policy was the NHS and Community Care Act 1990. Thereafter, hospital closures became major programmes, with resettlement of people with learning disabilities into the community in a range of different styles of living.

Social inclusion

Inclusion is a powerful concept that moves us on from 'participation' and 'integration' which both apply to someone from the outside being brought in, but not necessarily being totally absorbed or empowered. Social inclusion is based on the belief that societies need diversity and function best when the gifts of each individual are appreciated as contributing to the whole. So social inclusion is about citizenship, full membership and belonging. The social inclusion movement has used 'circles of support' to develop networks around individuals and stimulate the growth of mutually supportive communities. I shall return to circles of support later.

Individual programme planning

In the mid-1970s and 1980s the development of processes for planning with individuals was quite revolutionary. Lots of emphasis was being put on the need for people to have goals. Around this time an occupational therapist named Phoebe Caldwell was working with a long-stay hospital in Bristol to help people move out into the community. Some of the work that she carried out was recorded in a video called *Making Progress* in which she explained how she had enabled a group of men with very challenging reputations to develop skills and to eventually move on from institutional living to more valued lives. Phoebe Caldwell said in 1986, 'If you have no expectations you cannot achieve'. This is so very true, but people got confused between goals for individuals and goals for staff. As a result, lots of people end up with lives that are dominated by programmes designed to increase people's skills so that they can 'move on' to more independence. Here, we are clearly back to the 'readiness' model, with some people never seen as ready and so doomed to lives of dependency and failure. Initially, individual programme plans were thus often very service focused, which made it difficult for the person to break out and take control of their life.

Good practice in social work assessment

Assessment is the main tool of care managers for identifying the needs of a person so that a plan can be drawn up to address these needs. Care managers, however, have to work within resource limitations and there may well be a tension between a plan drawn up on person centred lines and the resources that are available. This can inevitably lead to compromise, disappointment and failure to fulfill expectations. Sanderson et al (1997) explain three models of assessment identified by Gerry Smull:

Questioning model: The professional asks questions based on previous experience in order to determine the correct 'diagnosis'. This is a clinical model, focusing on what is important to the professional, not the person.

Procedural model: The professional is still in control, but the process is based on allocation of resources once the person has been categorised against set criteria. This is very typical of care management processes.

Exchange model: This assumes that the person is the expert and engages the professional in problem-solving and negotiation. This is a model that reflects the role of the person centred planning facilitator.

For person centred planning to be successful the exchange model is favoured, but unless there is commitment within the organisation to allocate resources there is a risk of failure.

Valuing People

The White Paper *Valuing People*, published by the government in 2001, has changed the face of learning disability services in England for the 21st century. It is based on the four key principles of rights, independence, choice and inclusion. We shall return to this in a bit more detail later in this chapter.

ACTIVITY 2: **The medical and social models of disability**

Think of two people with learning disabilities that you know who, preferably, live in very different situations. Consider each one in terms of their current situation and where they lived or spent their time before – for instance someone living in their own tenancy now who previously lived in a group home, or someone with a variety of different daytime activities who used to attend a day centre. Compare their situations with those in Figure 2 and reflect on the model that applied. Hopefully, the social model applies now. If not, why not? What about the past? Were they seen as the problem and, if so, what impact did it have on their lives?

Now consider the following questions:

● Do the models help to clarify the impact of cultural attitudes on people's lives?

● Do you feel that the social model of disability influences the lives of the people you know today, or do people still, to a degree, perceive the person as the 'problem'?

● What changes could be made to alter this perception?

Comment

I hope that these questions have helped you to reflect upon the situation where you work and the lives of people you know. In particular, they may help you to think about your own role in challenging prejudice and discrimination and in how person centred planning can be used to empower the person with learning disabilities and help them to be fully included within society.

The differences between person centred planning and other approaches to care planning

Some common misconceptions are that:

- person centred planning is the same as assessment and care management

- person centred planning is another name for individual programme planning

- if you use the right proformas you are doing person centred planning

None of these is true. Let's take each of them in turn:

Assessment and care management: These are processes carried out by the care manager (a role created through the purchaser–provider split that was introduced by the NHS and Community Care Act 1990. Ideally, care management is driven by the same principles as person centred planning, but unfortunately the need for cost-effectiveness and financial accountability drive it towards a procedural model, rather than the exchange model, of assessment, as outlined earlier. Person centred planning is not an assessment, but assessment and care management should, ideally, be carried out in a person centred way.

Individual programme planning: This became very popular as people grasped ordinary life principles and looked for ways of helping people to develop their potential. It is very much a goal-focused approach, but the flaw is that staff and services, not the person, frequently set the goals. In consequence, they are often task focused rather than aspirational – for instance, 'learn to clean teeth unaided' rather than 'I would like to have a real job'. These are goals for staff by which to measure their own success rather than goals for the person to help them gain autonomy and control.

Proformas: There are lots of different styles for person centred planning, as we shall see later, but they are only there as flexible tools to help the person to focus on themself. When the plan has been written it is only just beginning. Some organisations have written their own set format for 'person centred planning' but this means that the person is often being fitted into a service-led system, rather than leading the process. Person centred planning is not about forms, it is about the person themself and what is right for them.

From all this it should be clear that person centred planning is *not*:

- assessment and care management
- individual programme planning
- a new form

It is also *not*:

- a checklist of abilities, or strengths and needs
- an assessment of skills for carrying out a particular task
- an annual review

These are all service-led approaches to determine someone's abilities, disabilities, skills and failures. Instead, person centred planning is:

- led by the person
- a way to help the person gain control over their life
- a way for the person to bring about change

Current legislation, government policies and guidelines

I have already briefly mentioned two important government policy documents:

- NHS and Community Care Act 1990 (England and Wales)
- White Paper *Valuing People: A New Strategy for Learning Disability for the 21st Century* that was issued in 2001 (applies to England only)

Some other important pieces of legislation in Britain that are relevant here are:

- Community Care (Direct Payments) Act 1996 (England and Wales)
- Human Rights Act 1998 (UK)
- Care Standards Act 2000 (England and Wales)
- Carers and Disabled Children Act 2000 (England and Wales)

There is a slightly different picture at times in Scotland, Wales and Northern Ireland. For instance, in Scotland there was a paper *Same as You? A Review of Services for People with Learning Disabilities* (Scottish Executive) instead of *Valuing People*, though many of the objectives are similar.

ACTIVITY 3: **Legislation policy and guidelines**

Using the Internet and other sources of information, list the main pieces of legislation that I have mentioned and write a short paragraph about each.

Then look up the Valuing People website (www.valuingpeople.gov.uk) and find out as much as you can about what Valuing People means for people with learning disabilities (the executive summary of the White Paper is useful here).

What can you find out about what is happening in your locality to implement Valuing People?

If you are in Scotland look up the Scottish Consortium for Learning Disability (SCLD) website (www.scld.org.uk). SCLD is an organisation set up to help people make the changes set out in *The Same as You?*, the Scottish equivalent to the *Valuing People* document.

What can you find out about what is happening in Scotland to implement the changes?

Comment

Implementation of Valuing People varies tremendously around the country. This is dependant largely on how successful the Learning Disability Partnership Board in the area has been at addressing the objectives and at working in partnership with other agencies and with people with learning disabilities and their carers in particular. A major stumbling block is the lack of additional funding to bring about change, but motivation and commitment can make a significant difference.

Other sources of help and guidance

It is important that you keep yourself up to date and continually develop your skills and knowledge in this fast-changing area of practice. This book cannot tell you everything, but the Internet is a wonderful resource for information and guidance. Two very useful websites which you can use to find out more about person centred planning are:

- Michael Smull and Friends: www.elpnet.net

- Paradigm: www.paradigm-uk.org

ACTIVITY 4: **Other sources of help and guidance**

Log on to the two websites given above to find out more about what is going on currently around person centred planning. Note that both websites have a range of papers available to download and links to other useful sites. See what you can find out to develop your skills and knowledge further.

Comment

Information and knowledge about person centred planning expands and develops every day as people learn from their own and other people's experiences. It is worth finding out what websites can be useful to you and logging on to them regularly to keep up to date.

Key points

- **Person centred planning has developed from approaches that aim to empower people with learning disabilities.**

- **Communities of practice share their expertise to enable inclusion and valued lifestyles.**

- **Person centred planning incorporates the social model of disability.**

- **The person, not the service, leads person centred planning.**

- **The government's White Paper *Valuing People* is based on the person centred principles of rights, independence, choice and inclusion.**

Chapter 2

Person centred planning styles

Introduction

As we have seen in the first chapter, person centred planning has grown out of work that people have done with people with learning disabilities in a whole range of situations. The most important thing is that person centred planning has been a way to enable the person at the centre of the process to take power and control over their life.

In this chapter we shall look at the different styles or techniques that have been developed and what makes each one special. We shall look at some examples of how person centred planning has been put into practice for different people. This will help you to reflect on why different styles are chosen, what aspects of their life are covered, how information is gathered, the roles of different people involved and how the process is evaluated. The main areas you will be helped to focus on are:

- the different styles of person centred planning

- how these styles compare and contrast with one another

- how the person with a learning disability is empowered to take the lead in their person centred plan

- how the organisation's complaints procedure relates to person centred planning

Person centred planning styles

Writers often talk about a 'family of approaches' that make up the range of person centred planning styles. Lyle O'Brien and O'Brien (2000) explain about the 'family tree' of eleven early approaches to person centred planning that developed. They point out how the similarities between these methods suggest that, just like in a real family, they share common genes, which are:

- focusing on the person rather than the disability

- using ordinary language

- actively seeking the person's abilities and 'gifts' in respect of their life as a member of the community

- strengthening the voice of the person and those who know the person best

As time went on, some of these different approaches developed further, while others fell by the wayside. We will focus on the five approaches described by Sanderson et al (1997), which are the main ones used in the UK:

- essential lifestyle planning

- individual service design

- personal futures planning

- MAP

- PATH

For each of these different styles we shall examine:

- origins and basis of the style

- what information is gathered

- how information is gathered

- when information is useful

- when information is not so useful

- particular features of the style

ACTIVITY 5: **Person centred planning styles**

Try to obtain a copy of *People, Plans and Possibilities: Exploring Person Centred Planning* by Sanderson, H., Kennedy, J., Ritchie, P. and Goodwin,G. (1997) published by SHS Ltd, Edinburgh. This book has some of the best accounts of different planning styles that are available. Read pages 88–127 before carrying on with the rest of this chapter.

Note that in person centred planning we talk about the person in the centre of the process as the 'focus' person.

Essential lifestyle planning

Origins and basis of the style: This is one of the most well known styles of person centred planning. It was developed by Michael Smull and Susan Burke-Harrison to assist people moving from institutional living into the community. Essential lifestyle planning (ELP) focuses on the person now, to help them to get a life that makes sense for them, but does not particularly help to focus on dreams and aspirations, although this can be added.

What information is gathered: the focus person's core beliefs, values and preferences.

How information is gathered: from the person, their family members, friends and others (including paid staff) who know and care about the person.

When information is useful: when the focus person is trying to bring about major change in their life – for instance, moving out of a group home or long-stay institution into their own home as tenant or homeowner.

When information is not so useful: when someone has a settled lifestyle that they are happy with, but wants to take on a new challenge, like getting a job or pursuing a new sport, activity or hobby.

Particular features of the style: Essential lifestyle planning looks at what is important in the focus person's life, takes account of their health and safety, develops a vision for the future and then mobilises service providers and resources to make it happen.

Figure 3: Essential lifestyle planning

Find out ...			... in order to ...
Non-negotiables	Strong preferences	Highly desirables	• discover the person's core values and preferences
People who really know and care about the person say ...			• account for the person's disability and safety
To be successful in supporting the person ...			
The person's reputation says ...			• develop a vision for the future
If this is going to happen we must ...			• mobilise and change community services
... listen to words and behaviour			

Taken from O'Brien and Lovatt (1992)

Daniel

Daniel lived in a residential home, which was due for closure. He was helped by his social worker to develop a circle of support that met with him and helped him to plan for his future. Together they established that he wanted to live with one particular friend, remaining in the city in which he lived now because all his life was there. Daniel was able to speak up well for himself and it was felt that this could be a really positive process for him. He led his own meetings and was pleased to feel that everyone listened to what he had to say and it was written down to make his plan. He was also realistic and accepted that there were limited resources so he might not get everything he wanted, but that the person centred planning process would help to achieve as much as possible for him to help to improve his life.

We shall meet Daniel again because there is much we can learn from his particular experience.

Individual service design

Origins and basis of the style: This style developed in a different way, from people trying to help service providers to understand and implement the principles of normalisation. It is based on trying to help people to empathise with the focus person and understand what it would be like to be them and to have experienced their history. This is then used to build up a picture of the person's needs and what is needed to meet them.

What information is gathered: the focus person's history.

How information is gathered: through a 'service design group' which is often a group of service staff who usually meet somewhere away from the service and are facilitated by someone independent.

When information is useful: when staff are struggling to understand the person or when there are not many people who know the focus person well.

When information is not so useful: when the person is known well and now needs help with focusing on dreams and aspirations.

Particular features of the style: Individual service design enables people to visit the past through the person's eyes and to develop key themes from which to extract the person's greatest needs. From this picture a plan can be developed to meet these needs.

James

This style of planning was used by people who worked with James. James is in his early forties and has lived in care situations for most of his life. When he came to live here he had a very negative reputation. However, staff realised that he had very little formal language with which to communicate as he was profoundly deaf, partially sighted and had autism. They helped him to learn how to use Makaton and objects of reference so that he could tell people what he wanted. He soon learnt to use these very effectively and became very much happier.

Staff then wanted to help him to have a person centred plan, but this was difficult as he knew few people outside the place where he lived. However, his parents were keen to be involved and helped staff to understand James's life and the traumas that he had coped with. Only then did they start to understand how disrupted his life had been as he was moved from one institution to another with only occasional visits home, and with his eyesight failing. The process enabled staff to think about how important it was for him to have his own space in his home and to look at all the ways that would help to enhance his communication skills.

James has lost his negative reputation completely, but people who support him know that he has a lot of energy and needs to have a very active lifestyle. As a result, he is a regular visitor to the local gym, goes to see his local football team play and enjoys walking and swimming. He also enjoys going out for a drive and to the local pub for a beer. He is happy and is respected by people who know him.

Personal futures planning

Origins and basis of the style: This style developed out of work on community development and planning, which was then applied to people with learning disabilities. It helps people to build on what is working well for the focus person now, and to look at what their dream would be for the future.

What information is gathered: an overview of the person's life (but not the day-to-day detail gathered by essential lifestyle planning), the person's abilities, 'gifts' and relationships.

How information is gathered: The focus person, their family and friends who are trying to engage unco-operative services may gather it. Alternatively, the service provider collaborating with the person and their circle, in order to deliberately challenge and change the service, may gather it.

When information is useful: when someone needs help to develop a vision; it is good for building partnerships between people involved in supporting the person, so that services can undergo positive change.

When information is not so useful: where more detail is wanted for major lifestyle change or where people already know about the person's life.

Particular features of the style: Of prime importance is the need for everyone to work together as equal partners to achieve change – see Figure 4 opposite, taken from O'Brien and Lovatt (1992).

MAP

Origins and basis of the style: Making action plans (MAPs) are planning styles that are used as tools to move from where the person is now to the future, involving the use of pictures or charts. They were originally developed for use with children to help them integrate into mainstream schooling.

What information is gathered: Several different charts are used to gather information about:

- the focus person's history

- their dreams

- their nightmares

- who they are, their character and personality

- their gifts, strengths and talents

- what the person needs in order to move away from the nightmares to achieve the dreams

- an action plan to get there

How information is gathered: A facilitated meeting is the usual way, involving the person and those who know and care about them. However, it can also be carried out on a one-to-one basis. Very often, it involves the formation of a circle of support which then gets involved in the problem solving needed to make the changes for the action plan to succeed.

Figure 4: Personal futures planning

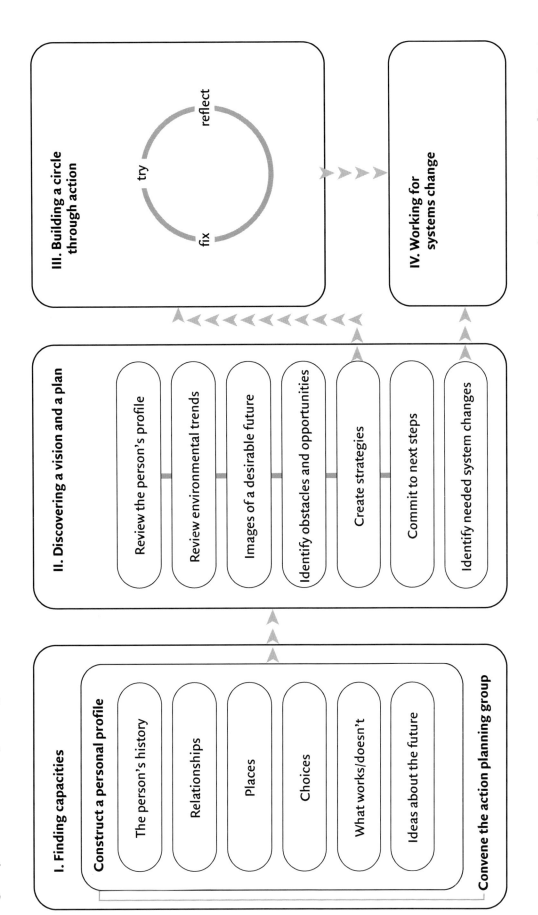

Taken from O'Brien and Lovatt (1992)

When information is useful: to help a person and their family to work towards a plan for the future that enables the person to move away from the nightmare and towards the dream; MAPs are somewhere between PATH (but not as focused) and essential lifestyle planning (but not as detailed).

When information is not so useful: when the person does not have a circle or people around who are supportive; it is also not so useful for someone who has not started to realise that they can dream.

Particular features of the style: This is a picture-building style of person centred planning, and the focus on gifts, strengths and talents can be instrumental in helping the person to make connections in the community.

Balwant

Balwant's circle spent a lot of time looking at his life with him. They drew different charts of his past, his morning routine, the different people he was close to, his best day and worst day. They discovered from the chart of people he was close to that those in the inner circle of most trusted people weren't the people that were with him the most, but two people who only helped out occasionally. He had no family and they realised that these two people represented family to him in being totally trusted and with whom he could share emotions. Going through his worst day and best day helped people to think about how Balwant was supported and to make sure that everyone knew what he needed and did not make assumptions. For instance, he hated noise, clutter and crowds and people making demands on him. He was getting older and losing his short-term memory, which was causing confusion some days.

An action plan was developed that made sure that his day was always shaped by how he felt, whether he felt able to join other people or whether he just wanted to stay quiet. People stopped making assumptions that it was not good for him to stay on his own and that he should go out, but learnt to respond instead to his needs on that particular day. His action plan was not about big life changes but enabled a change in the way he was supported as he got older, so that he could be happy and feel secure. As a result, he felt in control of his life and was able to relax and become more responsive to other people. The consequence of this was that people started to appreciate his talents more because they accepted him as he was. He had a wonderful sense of humour and musical ability and showed great warmth towards others.

PATH

The origins and basis of the style: Planning alternative tomorrows with hope (PATH) is a very focused style and is totally concerned with change. It was developed by O'Brien, Pearpoint and Forest as a planning style that could be used with individuals and with organisations (Kilbane and Sanderson, 2004) to enable a clear focus upon the future. Kilbane and Sanderson quote O'Brien and Pearpoint (2003) who explain that 'PATH is there when a situation is complex and will require concerted action, engaging other people and resources, over a longish period in order to make an important vision real.'

What information is gathered: PATH involves a facilitated meeting in which the person is helped to focus on their dream. The group firms up the person's vision for the future, identifies the difference between where they are now and where they want to be, and then works out how to get there.

How information is gathered: PATH is not an information gathering style.

When information is useful: This is a very useful planning style when there is a group of really committed people who know and care about the person and want to bring about change.

When information is not so useful: when people don't know enough about the person and need first of all to find out about their history, personality, gifts, strengths and talents.

Particular features of the style: PATH is a very dynamic planning style, concerned with planning direct and immediate action. It is more focused on the process of change than any of the other styles.

Nicky

Nicky's mum facilitated her plan and her circle included other family members, people who work with her now and people who have worked with her in the past but are no longer paid to do so. The plan was written down with pictures too, to help Nicky to understand it. The plan focuses on Nicky's wish to work with animals, her social life and on her future living independently from her parents. The planning process helped to clarify her needs and enabled her circle to put forward a clear case for support to meet these needs. For instance, instead of attending the day centre which was unable to meet her needs she now has the involvement of an outreach provider during the day. She has enjoyed a day trip to London, choosing to go with her outreach worker, who she sees as a friend, rather than her parents. She has also visited a nightclub, something she definitely would not have wished to do with her parents! She now goes to a local agricultural college two days a week, has a work placement at a farm, goes horse riding and is learning to care for horses. She is also learning the skills she needs to live in her own home, which is the ultimate goal.

ACTIVITY 6: **Planning styles**

Focus on two different people with learning disabilities that you know. Reflect on what you know about them, their lives, personalities, networks, talents, gifts. Then consider what planning style might suit each best. Make a note of:

● what style would suit them, and why

● why other styles are not suitable

● who might be able to get involved

● what their dreams might look like

● what problems might be experienced and how they could be surmounted (for instance, organisational restrictions, lack of funds, etc)

Try to choose a different style for each example.

Comment

Think about how easy it was to choose a planning style and whether, on reflection, you chose the right one. Did you find much difference in the way the two styles worked out? The exercise should help you to see how important it is to deal with facts and reality rather than assumptions about the person. In other words, you can't actually plan like this, in isolation from the person. They must be involved, together with the people who know and care about them, if the plan is actually to mean anything.

Key points

● There are five main styles of person centred planning used in the UK:

  ○ essential lifestyle planning

  ○ individual service design

  ○ personal futures planning

  ○ MAP

  ○ PATH

● Each style suits different circumstances for different people.

● All these styles belong to a 'family' of approaches that have some common principles.

The person at the centre

Crucial to person centred planning is the empowerment of the person with a learning disability to take the lead in the process.

> *'Power is an issue because many people are powerless. Their lives are controlled by others. Other people control in very direct ways how they spend their time, what they eat, how they behave, even what they say. In this context, planning can become just another indignity.'*

(Sanderson et al, 1997)

ACTIVITY 7: **Your person centred plan**

Think what it would be like for you to have a person centred plan. What would it look like, who would be involved and how could you make sure that you took the lead? Write an account that considers:

- what style you would use and why
- who would be involved and what role they would play
- how you would lead the process to ensure that it happened the way you wanted

Finally, reflect upon how someone with learning disabilities might be empowered to lead the process. What difficulties might be encountered and how could they be overcome? How different might their situation be from yours?

Write 800–1,000 words for this activity.

Comment

Some of the difficulties that you may have thought of, in enabling and empowering the person with learning disabilities to take the lead, could have been:

- the person's lack of confidence

- reluctance of others to let go of power and let the person take control

- no one available who the person can trust sufficiently to support them to lead the process

- problems for someone with high needs who does not understand the process

- failure of others to understand the person's communication

Clearly, the support of someone trusted is very important. This could be a family member, a friend, an advocate or even a paid worker. Without someone being there for the person, helping them to understand the process, communicate with others and lead their plan, they may encounter great difficulties.

Key tasks for this helper role will vary, depending on the needs of the person with learning disabilities, but may involve:

- helping the person to gather together a circle of support (more about this later)

- enabling the person to communicate in a way that others understand or advocating for them

- helping the person to understand what is going on

- pulling together resources or information

- finding out information to help the person know what options are available, for instance employment opportunities

---

ACTIVITY 8: **Empowerment**

Think back to the account you wrote in Activity 7. Now try to list the key things that enable the person to be empowered to lead their own planning process.

Comment

Each person will need different supports according to their individual circumstances. Formalised meetings may not be helpful or wanted, and the person may not actually be seeking major change in their life. However, I think that some of the important things that apply to anyone to make sure that they are central in the process and can take the lead in their own plan are:

- having someone to give *individual support*
- being given sufficient *time* to prepare and to understand
- being allowed a *choice* about who is involved and where and how meetings take place
- being *listened to*, and *heard*
- having the *information* that is needed
- being helped to *communicate* and to *understand* others
- having the focus on *abilities* and *success*, not disability and failure
- having respect for *confidentiality*, *privacy* and *dignity*
- having help to make the *plan happen*

Key points

- **The person must lead the process if person centred planning is to be successful.**
- **To do this, the person is likely to need individual support.**
- **Others must give away power to make this happen.**

When empowerment doesn't happen

This all sounds great. But what happens when it all falls apart? For instance:

- The person wants a person centred plan but is told that the service has its own system (which isn't person centred).
- The service says 'we do person centred planning' but the person has no say in the process.
- The planning looks good, but then nothing happens.

To illustrate this, we are again going to consider Daniel, who you met earlier in this section.

Daniel

Daniel lived in a residential home that was run by the local Hospital Trust. As part of their modernisation programme the home was planned for closure, although Daniel actually liked living there and saw it as his home. However, he accepted the inevitability of the situation and was pleased when he was told he would have help to write a person centred plan which would be used to help him to move to his own home. In his plan he made it clear that he wanted to live in the middle of the city with a particular person who was his friend and that he did not want to live on his own.

A new home was found for Daniel. It was a flat on his own, in a run-down estate on the edge of the city. He was invited to a meeting where this was explained to him. At the meeting he discovered that there had been several other meetings about the closure of the residential home, but he had not been invited. He was told that he could not live with the friend of his choosing since this was not part of his friend's person centred plan, and the flat that he was being offered was the only one available that was accessible to him because he used a wheelchair to get around. He felt that he had no alternative but to accept the flat offered because he was afraid of being put to live with someone he didn't like. He was promised that someone would be found to live with him because the flat did have two bedrooms.

Daniel felt angry and let down. He said that he understood that there might not be a place to live exactly where he wanted to be, but he had not been involved in the decision-making and promises had been made which had been broken. He decided that person centred planning was rubbish and didn't work.

I am sure that you can think of plenty of other similar scenarios when person centred planning doesn't happen and the person is still disempowered.

ACTIVITY 9: **Complaints procedures**

Find out about the complaints procedure of your organisation. Write a short account to explain how it works. Ask users of the service, their families, friends and staff about it, then answer the following questions:

- Do people with learning disabilities know about the complaints procedure?

- Do they and their families and friends know how to use it, and who they should tell about a complaint?

- Do people use it, and when they do, what happens?

- Is there any way in which the procedure, or its implementation, can be improved?

Comment

Every organisation should have an effective implemented complaints procedure. This is both a right and a need if people are to be empowered. You may, through this exercise, realise that the complaints procedure for your organisation is not as good as it could be, or is not implemented fully. If so, think about the action you can take to improve this situation – and do it now! It is essential that there is an effective and fully implemented complaints procedure in an organisation if the users of the service are to be able to speak out for change.

Key points

- **Empowerment relies upon an effective complaints procedure.**

- **The complaints procedure must be fully implemented.**

- **An implemented complaints procedure is both a right and a need of each person who receives services.**

Chapter 3

Skills and approaches

Introduction

I will now move on to consider the different roles that can be involved in developing and supporting person centred planning and the variety of skills that these roles embrace. This chapter will help you to focus on:

- the range of roles that can be involved in developing a person centred plan or supporting the process

- the skills needed to work with the focus person, their circle or people from other agencies

- the importance to the planning process of the focus person, their circle or people from other agencies

- how record-keeping and reports, anti-discriminatory practice and the promotion of equal opportunities are incorporated into the planning process, and how individual rights are upheld

- how the worker can use the risk assessment process to promote independence while fulfilling the organisation's duty of care

- how the individual worker can review and evaluate their involvement in person centred planning

Roles involved in the person centred planning process

Helper

If you look back to the previous chapter in the passage called 'The person at the centre' you will see that I discussed empowerment of the focus person and the important role of a trusted helper. This is the first role I will consider in this chapter, and it can be identified simply as the helper.

The helper may be a family member, a friend, a member of staff or an advocate. The important thing is that the person must be known and trusted by the focus person. This is a key role for both developing a person centred plan and ensuring that it is fully implemented. Looking back to chapter 2 you will see that the tasks of the helper may include:

- helping the person to gather together a circle of support

- enabling the person to communicate in a way that others understand, or advocating for them

- helping the person to understand what is going on

- pulling together resources or information

- finding out information to help the person know what options are available, eg employment opportunities

Facilitator

The focus person and their helper may need some support and advice in writing the plan. This can be given by the facilitator who might be able to advise how to ensure that the person remains at the centre of the plan, how to make sure that all parts of the plan really happen and deal with problems that arise. The facilitator might be a manager or a supervisor in a service, someone with the experience to give advice and guidance or someone who is in a position to influence other people and work across professional boundaries.

Advocate

If someone is not able to speak for themselves or has difficulty doing so, the important role of the advocate is needed so that the person's voice can be heard and they remain at the centre of the plan. An advocate must be committed totally to the person, so it is important to ensure that there is no conflict of interest. For example, if the advocate is employed by the agency that supports the focus person, or the agency which commissions the service for the person, they will have to abide by the agency's policies and procedures; realisation of the person's dreams may not be in the interests of the agency. Another example would be if the person wants to move from a group home to their own flat, the organisation running the group home would find themselves with a vacancy, so they might consider it preferable for the person not to move. If the keyworker is taking the role of advocate they will find themselves torn between the economic pressures of the agency and the wishes of the person. Clearly, an advocate needs to be completely independent, possibly employed by an advocacy organisation, or a friend or volunteer who is not paid by anyone and is totally committed to the person. Sometimes a family member can be an advocate, but it is also possible for someone in the person's family to believe they know what is best for them and to strive to achieve this, though it may not be what the person wants. This is definitely not advocacy.

Service manager

Person centred planning is not about services. However, most people with learning disabilities receive services and inevitably the co-operation of services is vital to ensure that plans really happen. Managers are crucial as they have the power to change services to ensure they meet the needs of the person and develop in a person centred way.

A lot of research in recent years has looked at why person centred planning isn't working. Peter Kinsella has written about this extensively, and his paper 'Barriers to Progress in Person Centred Planning' (2001), obtainable from the Paradigm website, talks about the importance of making sure that change is real and not just change in paperwork and the labels people use. He talks about person centred planning becoming a 'darling' of services, being used as a quality assurance tool with ambitious targets set for achievement. If person centred planning is to succeed it must be owned by the person, not by the service, but this means that services must be prepared to give up power.

There are other issues for managers which may on face value seem to contradict the principles of person centred planning:

- The manager must keep comprehensive records and reports that fulfil organisational or statutory policies and procedures.

- The manager has a 'duty of care' that may conflict with the person's wishes in their person centred plan.

To examine these issues I am going to pose you a scenario to focus on.

ACTIVITY 10: **Roles**

Kathryn has been writing her plan, assisted by her keyworker who is her 'helper'. In her plan she says that she wants to live on her own and to only have staff support for a short time in the morning and at night when she is getting her meals. She says that she does not want support during the day and that she wants to get a job and travel to work on the bus.

Kathryn has poor eyesight and a hearing loss. She has glasses and a hearing aid, but does not like wearing either as she thinks they look unattractive. However, without them she cannot see or hear traffic well enough to be able to travel across town safely.

You are the manager of the supported living scheme into which she is moving. What should you do in this situation?

Comment

Looking back at the two issues identified above, they both seem crucial in this situation. I hope you mentioned the need to conduct a risk assessment here. Risk assessment should be used as a tool to support responsible risk taking and promote independence safely. The key question in any risk assessment around someone's life therefore must be, 'What are the benefits to the person of taking the risk?' You will, of course, have considered who is at risk, what constitutes the risk and how the risk can be minimised.

In Kathryn's situation, the benefits of taking the risk are that:

- She feels more confident.

- She is able to travel on her own, which is her wish.

- She is able to get to work independently.

The risk is that she could have an accident and could even be killed.

In this situation you must balance the benefits against the risks and look at the crucial balance between your duty of care and her human rights. If Kathryn is able to make an informed choice she may insist on travelling alone, but you still have a duty to try to persuade her not to take an irresponsible or unacceptable risk. If, on the other hand, she lacks capacity to make this decision you must make a decision that is in her best interests and that abides by your duty of care. In this way you will uphold her right to protection and respect her human rights. However, there are many ways to do this. You and the staff could try different ways to persuade her that the glasses and hearing aid look really good. You could try to help her to have a better understanding of the risks. And so on. You will use your ingenuity to find a way to promote her independence and her rights without failing in your duty of care. Whatever actions you choose it is imperative that you:

- record all risk assessments and all decisions taken, and the reasons for them

- ensure that accurate records are kept to enable people to know how much support Kathryn needs, whether she is wearing her glasses and hearing aid, and so on

- review decisions regularly and monitor the situation

- keep records of all monitoring, reviews and evaluations

Finally, let's reflect on the point made by Sanderson et al (1997) that it is not just management that is needed but leadership. Leadership is 'focused on making a difference; management is simply running the organisation. Managers must also be leaders who can work in a person centred way themselves to act as champions and demonstrate real commitment to the people they serve.'

Person centred planning, when used as a management tool, becomes limited by resource allocation, which then breeds cynicism.

Figure 5: Person centred planning as a management tool

Kinsella, 2001

Look back to chapter 1 where I talked about good practice in social work assessment. Can you see how the concepts we are discussing here link back to the discussion about different models of assessment? As long as we stay with the procedural model of assessment, control and power remain with the professionals, 'management' and services.

How can this be changed? I believe that enlightened management is crucial to the success of person centred planning in services. A strong will to transfer power, courage to take risks and a commitment to allocate resources are necessary to ensure that real change happens.

Trainer

It is perfectly possible for someone to develop a successful person centred plan with a helper supporting them, but neither having had any training. This happens when the necessary supports are available, when the focus person knows what they want and when the helper is able to keep the person at the centre of the process because they believe that this is right. Often, however, it is not as easy as this. Many people are used to planning in ways that are not person centred and need help to understand the difference that person centred planning brings. Training is vital, not just for helpers, but also for facilitators, advocates and managers. So there is an important role here for the trainer to help change attitudes and enable people to have the skills and knowledge to take person centred planning forward.

ACTIVITY 11: **Barriers**

Log on to the Paradigm website at www.paradigm-uk.org and follow the links to articles about person centred planning (www.paradigm-uk.org/articlespcp.html) where you will find the article, 'What are the barriers in relation to person centred planning?' by Peter Kinsella, March 2001. Read this article and then consider, for the service in which you work:

- Who owns the process of person centred planning?

- Are there times when the service takes control and the person is left out? Be honest.

- Are there things that you can do to change this?

- What are the barriers for you in making this happen and can you do anything to reduce them?

Comment

I wonder if this was a difficult exercise to do? It is very hard to look at ourselves objectively, and we all want to believe that we are doing a really good job. However, if you were able to see some ways, even small ones, in which things could change you might take some very positive steps for the people you support.

Skills, abilities and attributes

You will have seen from the description of different roles that a range of different people may be involved in enabling the focus person to have a person centred plan. These may include:

- friends

- family members

- support workers from the person's home

- support workers from a day service

- managers

- advocate

- other professionals who are involved in the life of the person

- other people who are involved in a non-professional capacity (eg neighbours, colleagues) who may be members of a circle of support

---

ACTIVITY 12: **Skills, abilities and attributes**

Consider the skills, abilities and attributes that are needed to enable someone to have a person centred plan. Do you think that different skills are needed for different roles? Are there some skills, abilities and attributes that are needed by everyone who is involved?

Comment

I suspect that you will have decided that a range of skills is needed, depending on the role that the person is playing. For instance, a manager may need negotiating skills and the advocate will particularly need listening skills. However, I believe that there are core skills, abilities and attributes needed by everyone who is involved. I would list some of these as:

- empathy
- listening skills
- patience
- respect for others
- good communication skills
- determination
- trust

What is important is that a range of people who have these qualities will work together so that the focus person succeeds in developing and implementing their plan. There are two main groups of people who may be involved in enabling success for the person:

Enablers: These include members of the person's family, friends and other people who may belong to the circle of support. Their role is to bring energy, knowledge of the focus person and commitment to the process, and to enable it to move forward through partnership and trust.

Organisers: This group includes managers, other professionals and perhaps the keyworker. Their role is to bring expert advice, information and specific help and knowledge into the decision-making process. They are not expected to find all the solutions but can offer negotiating and communication skills to drive the process forward, or maybe just support the person by making sure that planning meetings are organised and chaired well.

Different people bring different qualities and all are important. It is worth noting the three 'nevers' proposed by Michael Smull in 1994:

- Never plan with someone you do not like.
- Never only plan once.
- Never plan without a commitment to implement the plan.

Anna

Anna is in her early fifties and has lived in a small residential home for the past eight years. The organisation that supports her has trained all support staff in person centred planning and now person centred plans are being developed by keyworkers for each resident. Anna's family do not want to get involved, she has few friends and she rarely goes out without a support worker. The process of developing her plan tended to consist of sitting with her keyworker who filled in a form to say what she would like to do and what support she needs to do this. The things in the plan were mostly about meals out with support staff or going shopping.

Meanwhile, the local Learning Disability Partnership Board had written a person centred planning action plan with a priority around enabling provider organisations to get involved in developing person centred plans. As a result, someone from social services, who introduced himself as a facilitator, came and spent some time with Anna and her keyworker. They talked about her networks, hopes and dreams and recorded these on large sheets of paper. Anna really seemed to enjoy this work but then suddenly refused to meet with the facilitator again and kept making excuses when he asked if he could visit Anna at her home. Eventually, the keyworker phoned the facilitator on Anna's behalf to say that Anna was finding the whole process very unsettling and was becoming depressed. She said that Anna had asked that the facilitator should not contact her again.

The issue that seems to present itself from this scenario is that person centred planning cannot be approached as a paper exercise, but must involve people who know the person well and are prepared to go at the person's own pace. It needs to be an ongoing process about the person's whole life and the agenda needs to belong to the person, not the professionals. They must work together to make it happen. Look back at the list of skills, abilities and attributes above. If people do not have these and just approach person centred planning as the latest model for planning, without the commitment that Michael Smull talks about, the plan will fail and people with learning disabilities will be let down yet again.

Key points

- **Several different roles are involved in person centred planning, with a range of skills.**

- **It is important to ensure that the focus person is always at the centre of the process.**

- **For person centred planning to succeed in services, managers need to be prepared to give away power, take risks and commit resources.**

Circles of support

I keep mentioning circles of support, so perhaps we should look at what is meant by this term. One powerful way to help someone to develop a person centred plan is by involving a group of people who know and care about them, to pool their knowledge of the person, their skills, networks and energy, focusing only on the person. The circle of support concept originated in North America but has been particularly championed in Britain by Circles Network in Bristol.

Mandy Neville, Director of Circles Network, describes a circle of support as:

> *'a group of friends invited by someone with a learning disability to*
> *get together regularly to plan, dream and act on that person's behalf.'*

> (Mandy Neville, 1996)

Note the use of the word 'friends'. A defining feature of a circle of support is that it is composed of a range of people such as: 'friends, family members, lovers, colleagues and neighbours. Sometimes human service professionals are included, but rarely would they be there in a paid capacity' (Neville, 1996).

Ben

Ben is 25 and has lived in various institutions since he was a teenager. He feels that many decisions in his life have been taken by others. Because of this, he found it difficult to plan when he first moved into the community and only tended to think in terms of services. His advocate found out about training for people who wanted to set up person centred plans and supported him to attend the course over a number of weeks. Ben enjoyed the training and talked about who might be in his circle and how he could record his plan.

Ben decided he would facilitate his own meetings and, with support from his advocate and facilitator, took responsibility for choosing venues, contacting people to agree dates, sending out invitations and taking notes. He invited seven people apart from the advocate to be in his circle. These were all people who were or had been paid to work with him and included his social worker and community nurse. Ben had a large network of friends and contacts in his local community but was very clear that he did not want to invite them to his meetings. He felt it was 'his business' and did not want to share it with them. Ben also wanted to be in control of his plan and set it up as a PowerPoint presentation on his computer with photos of circle members, notes and decisions recorded on it. The facilitator helped with mapping and other sessions to graphically record Ben's dreams and hopes and also helped him to think of supports and not just services. However, these are seen by Ben as separate from his plan – something to help him think about what he wants to do.

There have been some really positive results from his circle and Ben's leadership has taught professionals to work in different ways. Initially, he could sometimes abuse the power he had gained, for example by embarrassing people who arrived late, but some good working partnerships have now developed between circle members and Ben. Not everyone comes to every meeting and Ben has involved new people. For instance, a direct payments worker who gave Ben the information he needed to explain about direct payments to the rest of the circle. The circle has also given Ben the opportunity to redefine his relationship with someone who had worked as his support worker in the past, but now was in the circle unpaid, out of choice.

Ben is increasingly trying to replace specialist learning disability services with community support and his circle meetings give him the opportunity to explore different possibilities. For example, his social worker wanted to refer him to a supported employment scheme but during a circle meeting he was prompted to think about his own networks and realised that he knew very well the owner of several local hotels who he could approach for himself to ask about part-time work.

ACTIVITY 13: **Circles of support: power**

Using the example of Ben, consider the following questions:

● Do people have to be at a meeting to be part of your circle of support?

● How do we support people to facilitate their own meetings and record plans?

● What difference would it have made if the circle had been made up of people who were not paid to work with Ben?

● Why is it difficult to develop a circle of 'friends' in the way described by Mandy Neville?

Comment

The chances are that you have concluded that circles are not easy to form and often do not really consist of 'friends' if we are being honest.

Time and again a circle will be composed perhaps of family members, maybe one or two non-family people known to the person but not paid to be there, and a number of staff and professionals. Why? No doubt you concluded that people with learning disabilities often have limited networks, have difficulty making and maintaining relationships and frequently do not have 'colleagues' in work or college. The alternatives then are no circle or a compromise involving the people who are around and do care about the person, even though they are paid staff.

Does it matter? I think it does. A key point made by Mandy Neville is that a circle of support is 'a vehicle for advocacy' (Neville, 1996). Advocacy means 'speaking for', but there is a real danger that the well-meaning intentions that staff may have to speak for the person will be subverted by their need to comply with organisational policies and procedures, or by conflicting pressures from management. We have explored this area already, under the role of 'advocacy'. However, in the face of the alternative, when someone has few or no friends who could make up a circle, maybe the compromise is better than nothing. We should not be complacent, though, and surely there is a real priority in the need to help the person to extend their network of friends. The aim is to assemble a group of people to focus on the person 'as an equal, to enable the person to dream and achieve those dreams' (Neville, 1996).

ACTIVITY 14: **Circles of support: skills**

Consider someone you know who could benefit from a circle of support. What are the skills that you would need to enable the person to bring together their circle, and for you to support the circle to develop a person centred plan with the person?

Comment

If a circle of support is to be successful a manager's skills in this situation are very important. Of course, there are many ways of going about this task, but I would suggest that some of the skills needed must be:

- advocacy
- listening
- co-ordination
- diplomacy
- communication
- motivation
- facilitation
- reflection

There are lots of similarities here to the roles of the person centred planning helper and facilitator, so take a look back at the earlier part of this chapter to remind yourself.

Working with people from other agencies

Too often in the past workers have worked in isolation from others. Even if a range of professionals has been involved in someone's life it is not unusual for someone to be helped to develop a person centred plan in the place where they live, while another group of staff develop another (and different) plan where the person spends their day. How can these plans be person centred if neither plan encompass the whole of the person's life? We must remember that:

- A team involves everyone, including the person themselves and their family and friends.

- No one has ownership of the plan except the person themselves.

- Strength derives from co-operation, sharing and communication, not from competition, power struggles and distrust.

- Person centred planning involves partnership, which can overcome inequality, powerlessness and dependency.

Anti-discrimination and equal opportunities

A shared approach has other benefits too. Helping somebody overcome barriers to inclusion and to become a full citizen in their own right is often an enormous challenge. Not only may the person need a lot of new skills, particularly around communication, but also they may be up against discrimination born of ignorance, fear and restrictive social pressures. A team approach in which trust is built up across traditional boundaries can enable barriers to be broken down, discrimination to be challenged and equal opportunities upheld.

Rahina

Rahina had attended a day centre for many years and it was assumed that she could not work because she had learning disabilities. However, the day centre started to try to help people into employment and Rahina was given the support of Laura who helped her to develop a person centred plan. Rahina had always liked cooking and wanted to work in a kitchen. Laura investigated the different agencies in the area. She found an old people's home that was prepared to offer Rahina a placement in the kitchen. She did so well that she was offered a paid job and was given support to study for an NVQ. Rahina managed to gain her NVQ certificate in kitchen skills and she also developed a relationship with Dipak who worked with her. Dipak moved in to live with her and as Rahina overcame discrimination and prejudice her confidence grew immeasurably.

This example shows that, with support and encouragement, society's barriers can be overcome. Person centred planning can be used as a vehicle to discover a person's aspirations and then enable them to gain the skills needed to achieve. However, support and persistence may be needed to ensure that equal opportunities are observed. Sharing the goals with the focus person means that the circle takes on this responsibility rather than the person on their own. Once again, this is about teamwork, communication, co-operation and shared enterprise.

Review and self-evaluation

ACTIVITY 15: **Personal reflection: skills and approaches**

Develop a reflective journal of about 500 words of your own role in the development of a person centred plan and the ongoing implementation of the plan. Ensure that this journal addresses all the issues listed in the introduction to chapter 3 (explaining what different roles might be involved and the particular role that you have played on this occasion).

Finish your journal with an evaluation of your contribution and suggestions for how this could be improved.

When you have finished, add the journal to your portfolio to give evidence towards the LDAF Level 4 award.

Comment

You are no doubt well aware of the need to keep your performance under regular review and to evaluate how you are doing. Some other ways in which you can do this might be to:

- gain feedback from the person themselves

- check with members of a person's circle and gain their feedback on the process

- use your own supervision to discuss your involvement in person centred planning

- use training and development opportunities to help you to reflect on your role

- actively encourage and become involved in team discussion that gives honest feedback

Remember, no one ever gets it all right all of the time. We can always learn, but only if we are ready to listen, accept and grow.

Key points

- A circle of support is a vehicle for advocacy to enable someone to dream and achieve their dreams.

- Person centred planning involves partnership that can overcome powerlessness and dependency.

- Team working enables strength, sharing and communication.

- Person centred planning can be a tool to overcome inequalities and discrimination in society.

- It is important for workers to evaluate and review their role to ensure that their contribution to person centred planning is effective.

Chapter 4

Barriers and challenges

Introduction

'The origins of most person centred planning lie outside of services' (Kinsella, 2001). However, in Britain it is most usual for person centred planning to be led by staff and professionals in services rather than people with learning disabilities or their family carers, with resultant tensions and limitation to progress.

In this chapter you will be helped to focus on:

- some of the main organisational and structural barriers to person centred planning

- the challenges and conflicts faced by services

- ways of overcoming these barriers to enable individual success

Organisational structures and barriers

In the last chapter (Activity 11) you were directed to the article, 'What are the barriers in relation to person centred planning?' written by Peter Kinsella in 2001 which you will find on the Paradigm website. Before proceeding, return to this article and read it through again, and then tackle Activity 16.

ACTIVITY 16: **Organisational structures and barriers**

Consider the organisation that you work for and then, reflecting on Peter Kinsella's paper, write about 800 words on the structures and barriers that exist within the organisation. Explain what they are and analyse why they exist.

Comment

It is often difficult to be critical or objective about one's own situation. However, you may have come up with some of the following structures and barriers:

Funding: The funding available is often very limited and may result in limited staff resources, complicated procedures for accessing money for activities and money being tied up in buildings and equipment. Funding will be to a set amount, determined by a rigid budget and service-led goals. It is not flexible enough to be used in imaginative ways to meet individual aspirations and is frequently insufficient to provide support at the times people need.

Buildings: Services become focused on places and buildings rather than people. This makes it hard for someone to assert their independence because the building acts as a straightjacket and becomes very important, with activity centred upon the needs of the building rather than the people in it.

Staff rotas: Staff frequently work to a set rota of early and late shifts. However, if the person wants to react spontaneously and do something interesting and exciting there are often too few staff on duty to support them to do it. Of course, the reverse of this situation has flaws too – staff want to know when they are working and when they are off duty so that they can have a social life. If this is denied in the name of flexibility we are in danger of coming full circle to the situation that often prevailed in the 1960s and 1970s when staff were expected to live on site and be available whenever needed, eating communally and with a small bedsit for accommodation. Consequently they had no social life, apart from the other people they worked with, and became institutionalised themselves – not good role models or supporters for anyone striving for inclusion.

Policies and procedures: Organisational policies and procedures are written to ensure that staff have a framework within which to work, but these can restrict practice too and may present staff with a conflict between the wishes of the person and the requirements of the organisation. However, they are employed by the organisation to which they are therefore answerable and so must abide by policies and procedures.

Business objectives of the organisation: If the organisation does not put people first in its strategic planning, the experience of people with learning disabilities will be affected and staff will be unable to deliver a person centred service. In other words, person centred services must be led from the top down and championed by the people who control resources.

Documentation: An organisation may claim to do person centred planning and design forms called person centred plans which are actually little more than redesigned individual programme plans and goal plans (with goals set around what staff think are best, not what the person wants). They may also adopt one form of person centred planning (this often happens with essential lifestyle planning) and follow it slavishly, rather than helping each person to have a plan designed around their personal requirements. Off-the-shelf planning makes for off-the-shelf plans which lose sight of the individual but look very impressive and help staff to feel that they are achieving.

Person centred planning as an organisational tool: Plans may be seen as a goal in themselves, to be quantified as a performance indicator. Thus the planning process fulfils service objectives and the content of individual plans becomes irrelevant.

Segregated services: Because services encourage segregation and group existence, the aspirations of many plans remain just that – dreams which will never be realised. Too seldom do people manage to escape from the service structure, to advocate for themselves, control their own funding (through direct payments) and the way they live.

Lack of motivation: Person centred planning is of necessity a slow process if it is to be designed around the person and at their pace. However, the consequence can be a loss of momentum, demotivated staff who do not see immediate results and loss of faith and trust of people with learning disabilities who feel let down yet again.

Lack of leadership: This is a crucial element to making person centred planning a success, person by person, step by step, regardless of barriers and constraints. A committed, highly motivated leader can inspire others, lead them in developing the skills they need and help them to keep sight of the real goal, which is that of person centred approaches for each and every person.

That's my list, but you may have more. The message that comes over clearly, I feel, is that it is very difficult to make person centred planning work in services and inevitable in Britain that this is where it happens. Efforts must be made therefore to overcome these barriers and organisational structures to help person centred planning to succeed.

Key points

- **Person centred planning requires a fundamental shift of power.**

- **Organisations must put people first in their strategic planning for person centred planning to be effective.**

- **Change must be led from the top.**

- **Resources need to be flexible to enable services to become person centred.**

Challenges and conflicts

Routledge and Gitsham (2004) list the challenges faced by agencies and organisations stemming from the barriers discussed above. They talk about:

- superficial, rather than real changes

- training for staff but not families or people with learning disabilities

- a focus on processes rather than outcomes, which may be at an individual or a strategic level, or both

- a disconnect between resource allocation and person centred planning, with a lack of connection with the care management process

- the focus of training being on the planning process but not implementation, support systems, monitoring, review and evaluation with the result that person centred planning fails to be embedded into the culture of the organisation

- person centred planning being implemented in isolation and therefore not linked in with the other plans and strategies that are being taken forward by Learning Disability Partnership Boards

- Valuing People identifying priority groups (people in transition from children's to adult services, people using large day centres, people living on NHS residential campuses, people in long-stay hospitals and people living with older carers) but few people in these groups being able to access person centred planning

- a lack of coherence or co-operation between agencies which are not working in partnership, and incompatible cultures, structures and planning systems which may ultimately fail to deliver the required outcomes

---

ACTIVITY 17: **Managing challenges**

Look back at the example of Daniel described in chapter 2. If you recall, Daniel had been involved in the initial planning process, but the outcome for him was very unsatisfactory. Re-read Daniel's story and then consider the following questions:

- What caused the situation in which Daniel's expectations were not met?

- How could the situation now be managed?

- How could things have been managed better in the first place?

Comment

There are many possible causes for Daniel's unhappiness but the main one would appear to be lack of involvement, with people not consulting him, listening to him or respecting his views and wishes. He ended up with a total compromise, and maybe all that could have been done subsequently was to try to make it work for him by supporting him through the process and listening to him properly. You may have felt, however, that it was still not too late to return to the drawing-board, to try to find out what Daniel's friend really wanted (had he not been heard properly either?) and maybe, just maybe, fulfil Daniel's dream. Of course, hindsight is always wonderful, but I think people really could have done a better job here. If Daniel had been involved in all meetings and discussions, if he and his friend had been supported to discuss what they wanted together, if he had had active support to go out and look at possible flats, there might have been a better outcome. There would, however, have been resource implications here:

- There might have been quite a lot of staff time needed to take Daniel through the process, though perhaps a volunteer could have been found to act as an advocate.

- Adaptations might have been necessary to make the chosen flat accessible. This could have been costly but perhaps a grant could have been found to help.

- The whole process might have taken longer with implications for the time of all paid workers involved.

The principle here must be to try. If we find accommodation suitable for someone who uses a wheelchair and then look for someone to fit it, or if we limit our horizons regarding the kind of places we are prepared to consider, then the process will never be person centred. Person centred planning needs us to think imaginatively, try new concepts and take considered risks. If we do not, then empty promises will continue to be made.

Carl

One of the staff at the residential home where Carl lived was chosen as his facilitator to help him to develop a person centred plan. His keyworker, brother, advocacy group supporter and a volunteer at the home who had known Carl for a long time were chosen as his circle. The first meeting was to be held at the lounge in his home and invitations were sent out from Carl inviting people to his meeting.

At the first meeting other residents wandered in and out of the lounge, Carl's brother turned up nearly an hour late and Carl felt excluded from lengthy discussions about a new wheelchair and other things he 'needed'.

A second meeting was held and Carl's brother did not turn up at all. The circle used pictures to allow Carl to choose what to talk about and he indicated that he would like to go on holiday. The circle was very enthusiastic about this and fired a large number of questions at Carl to find out when, where and how he would like to go and who he would like to go with. Carl reacted to this by becoming increasingly distressed and making it very clear that he didn't want the meeting to continue.

At this point, it was important to rethink the whole process and a volunteer facilitator was introduced. She suggested working with Carl on making sure people took notice of what he said – for example, the way he indicated his personal care needs and the people he really liked working with. It became clear that it was difficult for Carl to choose from the large number of people working at the home. A 'talking photo album' was bought which had 24 plastic pockets and a button on each page which could be pressed to record a short message. The volunteer facilitator and Carl's keyworker took photographs of Carl indicating his needs, feelings and preferences and of the people he met at the home, day centre and at other activities. Short messages were recorded under each with Carl indicating when he was happy with what had been said. Carl was clear that he wanted to keep the album in the bag on the back of the wheelchair, and an ID-type card was produced on the computer to let people know that Carl had something to say and that the album was in his bag. Carl liked the idea of wearing the card around his neck and had enough movement in his thumb to indicate the card and draw attention to it. Carl started to use the album to indicate people who he liked or who had upset him and, over time, it is hoped that this will help him choose members of his circle. One of his long-term aims is to move and the next step will be to start to collect evidence of people, places and things that are important to him.

One day the volunteer called into the day centre that Carl attends and noticed that he was not wearing his card and that the album was not in his bag. She discovered that his keyworker at the centre knew nothing about them and that the member of staff from his home who supported Carl at his annual review with his social worker had forgotten to take along the album.

ACTIVITY 18: **Organisational challenges and conflicts**

Having read the example of Carl, think about the problems that were experienced and how they could be overcome. In doing this, consider the answers to these questions:

● What makes a good venue for a person centred planning meeting? Did Carl choose to meet in the lounge because he didn't understand the options?

● How can you make someone feel that it is their meeting if they do not use words to communicate and everyone else in the circle does?

● Why did staff fail to ensure that the book was in Carl's bag and that he had his card with him? Why did staff at the day centre not know about it?

Comment

Although the issues are particular problems on a individual level, they are likely to be symptomatic of failure on an organisational level, for example the lack of inter-agency communication, the need for staff skills development around communication needs of people with learning disabilities, and the need to involve family members in person centred planning training. Unless person centred approaches are incorporated within the culture of the organisation, person centred planning will be an 'add-on', seen in isolation from other processes and doomed to failure.

Overcoming challenges and conflicts

Clearly, challenges and conflicts on an organisational level need to be tackled in a strategic way, since intervention on an individual level may only address the symptoms, but not the causes. However, Routledge and Gitsham (2004) talk about the importance of organisations learning strategically through planning and making changes around individuals. They talk about the need to adjust how resources are used and make changes to management and recruitment practices. They point out that it is crucial that services look carefully at what people are saying in their person centred plans and how this differs from what services are actually doing. Addressing the culture of services and changing the way that resources are allocated must impact upon these differences. This then increases their capacity to be responsive to people's wishes. Thus there needs to be a balance between the investment in developing person centred plans and the investment in capacity development through service change. The following diagram may be useful in summing up this concept.

Figure 6: The strategic context for person centred planning

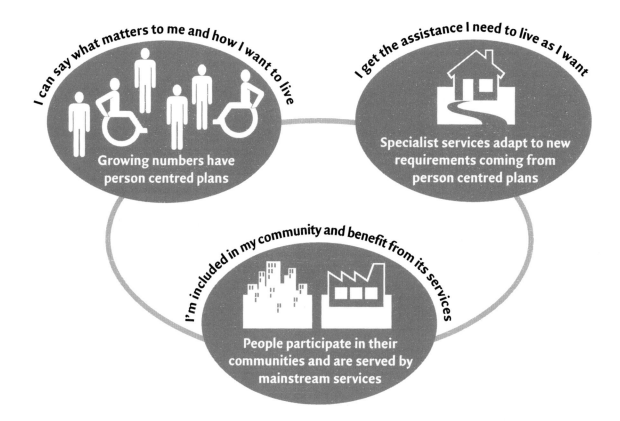

Routledge and Gitsham, 2004

Routledge and Gitsham suggest that investment is needed in:

- training and practical help for families and people with learning disabilities so that they can become involved in planning

- enough person centred planning facilitators to support them

- plans that target the priority groups highlighted in *Valuing People*

- efforts to ensure that there are strong connections between person centred planning and other Partnership Board strategies

- culture change for specialist providers to bring about fundamental change at both an organisational and individual level, with changes in resource allocation and management processes

These themes are echoed by Sanderson et al (1997) who say that person centred planning for someone who relies heavily on services will only be successful if five essential criteria are met:

- There is someone really committed to change (the person themselves, or a member of staff or, preferably, a family member or someone independent of the service) to champion the person's plan.

- There is a skilled facilitator to guide the process and ensure that the person remains central to it.

- The person has the support of a committed group of people with 'shared purpose and passion', preferably some of whom are not accountable to the organisation.

- There is an effective team manager who is committed to the person and empowered to make shifts in the ways that staff are deployed and to enable inclusion. This may well involve a change in the way decisions are made within the organisation.

- The service is committed to change at a strategic level so that it is prepared to make cultural, policy and resource changes.

ACTIVITY 19: **Overcoming challenges and conflicts**

Referring back to the structures and barriers that you considered in Activity 16 and reflecting on what you have learned in this section, consider what challenges and conflicts they present you with and how you could overcome them. Write about 500–800 words on this and then try to develop an action plan to help you to start to tackle them.

Comment

You may have found it difficult to develop the action plan, particularly as change at a strategic level may be out of your control. However, do try to look at ways in which you can raise awareness in your organisation and start the process of change. On the other hand, you may already be a good way along this road, in which case congratulations but keep going. What is important is that we face up to the conflicts and challenges honestly so that person centred planning can become a reality for people with learning disabilities.

Here are two examples that demonstrate practical ways in which an organisation can create an environment that supports person centred planning and person centred approaches. First of all, we shall consider the story of James again.

James

James is profoundly deaf and has limited sight. He also has autism and finds it difficult to communicate what he wants. This can result in great frustration for him and he will hit his head and shout when he is not happy. However, when he moved to his current home staff helped him to learn to use Makaton to communicate and soon he learnt how to ask for activities that he enjoys, food that he likes and so on. As a result, his frustration declined and he became much happier.

An eye test showed that James's sight was deteriorating rapidly and that he would probably go completely blind. Staff met with his mother and health professionals and drew up a plan to make sure that he would still be able to communicate clearly when he could no longer see enough to use Makaton. They taught him to use 'objects of reference' so that he could find the object representing what he wanted and show it to staff. They also taught him to track his way around his house, finding landmarks that enabled him to know where he was.

Luckily, the eye specialist decided that he might be able to save James's sight with an operation. This was a new worry as James did not like anyone touching his face and it was felt by health professionals that it would probably be unwise to proceed with the operation as James would not tolerate eye drops or a shield on his eye. His staff and his mother were determined that he should have the chance to get some of his sight back. They helped him to get used to the hospital by going there frequently just to visit. They carried out a desensitisation programme using drops of water until he allowed drops in his eyes without becoming upset and they went with him to the hospital and stayed while he had his operation and recuperated. The operation was a success. James accepted the medical intervention and he can now use Makaton again to communicate, though he likes to also use his objects of reference to get his message across even more clearly. He has bought himself a bubble tube and fibre optics for his bedroom where he likes to go to relax. He is active, happy and relaxed and has chosen to take part in a range of activities, including going to the pub and the gym. He gets involved in preparing meals and seldom shouts or hurts himself.

The whole process took hours of staff time. They changed the way they worked, altered the environment to suit James's needs, involved lots of other people to help and listened carefully to James's mother. This wasn't just about writing a plan, it was person centred approaches in action.

William

William has lived for twelve years in a bungalow with five other people. Some of the staff have known him all that time. He has no family at all. William uses signs to communicate as he does not use verbal language. William has Down syndrome and has now developed dementia. Health professionals are doubtful whether the service can go on meeting his needs, but the staff disagree and are determined that he should stay living in the home in which he is happy. The whole team are very committed and have got together and developed a person centred plan for William.

William's plan is not about moving house, getting a job or the kind of thing that many people focus on. It is about making sure that he understands what is happening and that he feels happy and secure. Staff have done a lot of work to find out about his past and are using that knowledge to help him to do things that make sense to him. For instance, they have helped him to get a CD player so that he can listen to some of the music that he enjoyed years ago. He finds the disruption of a holiday away from home quite traumatic so they have thought about the kind of places he enjoys visiting and have arranged a series of day trips instead. He finds these much more enjoyable because he always comes home at the end of the day. The manager has negotiated with William's funding authority who have agreed to additional staff hours to enable him to have the level of support he needs to feel safe in his home, which is very important to him. This sometimes means someone just being with him in his room for several hours in the morning to help him to gradually get up and start his day. Without this support he gets upset, becomes distressed and loses the confidence to come out of his room. However, once he is up he can enjoy his day, playing music and even joking and laughing with people.

In this way, person centred approaches are helping William to have real quality of life. This is not an exciting story about fundamental change, but then a lot of people's lives are not like that. It is about helping someone to have the life he wants, where he wants it, in the place he knows as home, with the people who know and love him. It is possible because it is led by the manager who has motivated the whole team and has kept William as the priority throughout.

Key points

- **Strategic direction needs to be steered by individual planning.**
- **Change requires a shift in management systems and procedures.**
- **A balance is needed in the investment in person centred planning and the investment in capacity development through service change.**
- **Person centred planning at the individual level will only be successful if there is commitment at all levels and from everyone involved.**

Chapter 5

Funding and resources

Introduction

All the way through this book references have been made to resource availability.
I have mentioned staffing, advocacy, support, information and, most of all, money.
Money is, as we all know, an essential factor in life that enables us to obtain the
things we need, and it is crucial for the success of person centred planning.

This chapter will help you focus on:

- the ways funding is allocated on both local and national levels

- how allocation impacts upon availability of resources of all kinds

- how people can report shortfalls in resources to try to bring about change

Allocation and distribution of funding

Funding may come from a variety of sources, depending upon the nature of the
service, how it is set up, where the person is living, how much help they may need
with getting around, and so on. This complicated picture has built up as a result
of various different pieces of legislation, regulations and policies and can be very
difficult to understand.

ACTIVITY 20: **Funding**

Think about the service in which you work and how it is funded. (If you are a budget holder this may be a very easy exercise for you, but if not talk to your manager to find out what you need to know.) From your enquiries, try to answer the following questions:

- If you deliver direct services to individuals with a learning disability, where does the funding for each person come from and how is it calculated?

- Does your agency receive any grants that benefit the individuals you support?

- What other funding does your agency receive that contributes to the support of individuals?

Comment

This activity will probably have highlighted that funding is very complex, beset by regulations and often inadequate for the needs of the person. It also varies around the country and is calculated against different formulae depending on where you happen to be and what type of agency you work in.

I will now look at this whole complex situation to try to tease out the main issues, reviewing the background of legislation and national policy.

NHS and Community Care Act 1990

No doubt you are familiar with this piece of landmark legislation which I have already referred to in chapter 1. The NHS and Community Care Act 1990 is one of the most important pieces of social care legislation to be enacted in recent years, the main objectives being:

- to promote the development of services which enable people to live in their own homes wherever possible

- to ensure that practical support for informal carers is a priority

- to make a proper assessment of need at an individual level

(Hughes, 1995)

The Act has resulted in the purchaser–provider split in which local authorities, social authorities and health authorities have become the commissioners of care packages delivered by a range of providers that constitute the health and social care market-place. A new role has also emerged through this structure – the care manager has budgetary responsibility for care packages designed around assessed needs. This person contracts with the service provider and acts as the co-ordinator for all involved in the service package and therefore plays a key role here in ensuring that the package is person centred. But there are tensions involved:

- The care manager operates within budgetary limitations and so there is a tendency to adopt the 'procedural' model of assessment as outlined in chapter 1. This means that assessment takes place against set criteria in order to determine eligibility for services. These criteria are liable to give a very narrow view of care needs, concentrating on basic physiological needs such as personal care, eating, drinking and sleeping. More individual areas of need such as self-respect, combating loneliness and providing social stimulation can be overlooked, leading to a minimalist care package that is far from person centred.

- Care management can be a slow process, bogged down by procedures and the barriers imposed by organisational structure. Once needs have been assessed it can be difficult to bring about change for the person as their file is closed and the case will only be reopened if there is a significant change in needs. Moreover, a reviewing officer instead of the original care manager often carries out reviews so there is a danger of assumptions being made (often based on philosophical or political dogma rather than on knowledge of the person) and the co-ordinating role being lost.

- The care management system frequently results in the person being just as disempowered as before, with power simply shifting from the service provider to the purchaser.

Community Care, Services for Carers and Children's Services (Direct Payments) Guidance England 2003

The government introduced direct payments in 1997 as a way of giving people control over their lives. Under this scheme, instead of the local authority purchasing services for the person, money is given directly to the person so that they can choose and buy the services they want. Social services still carry responsibility for ensuring that assessed needs are met, but power for implementing this responsibility transfers to the person themselves. Thus the key features of direct payments are power, control, choice and flexibility. However, there are also drawbacks. The government have been very disappointed by the slow take-up of direct payments among people with learning disabilities. This has often been because people do not believe that people with learning disabilities can manage direct payments and they may not have access to advocacy support to enable them to do so. They may also have difficulty understanding how direct payments work and may have insufficient information to support them. There are also concerns about the lack of regulation of support staff who are employed under direct payments, with possible increased risk of abuse to the person buying the service. Employing staff is not easy and many people with learning disabilities may need considerable support to do this. Finally, it must be remembered that the amount of money available under direct payments is no different from that held by the care manager who arranges a care package – no more funding is available through this route.

The government maintains its commitment to increasing the take-up of direct payments and a realisation appears to be dawning that more needs to be done to ensure that direct payments are a real choice for people everywhere. For example, people employing their own personal assistants do not have access to the Criminal Records Bureau or the protection offered by the Protection of Vulnerable Adults (POVA) list. There are also barriers imposed by taxation and all the practicalities of becoming an employer which need to be addressed (Jerrom, 2004).

Supporting people

In 2003 the Supporting People programme was launched with the aim of 'providing a better quality of life for vulnerable people to live more independently and maintain their tenancies' (Office of the Deputy Prime Minister, 2004). The programme has four objectives:

- to deliver quality of life to promote independence

- to enable high-quality and cost-effective services

- to develop services that are needs led

- to support partnership between service users and a range of agencies

Supporting People is relevant to a wide range of client groups, among which are people with learning disabilities. It offers housing-related support which aims to encourage independent living within the community. It is thus a key factor for supported living, a term used for living arrangements in which the person has either a tenancy agreement or is a property owner, with support being provided by an independent agency. Separation of housing and support is a key factor in supported living that enables greater flexibility and empowerment for the person who has control over where and how they live instead of having to adapt and fit into a placement in residential accommodation.

Supporting People funding has replaced some finance previously accessed through the benefits system such as housing benefit. It is managed by the Local Authority Social Services Department but is totally separate from finance available for personal care support. The advantages of Supporting People are that it is:

- responsive to the needs of the person

- designed to promote choice and autonomy

- a way of enabling people to escape from residential living

The disadvantages are that it:

- has cost far more than the government anticipated (particularly for people with learning disabilities) and may result in some services losing their funding in the future if they can be seen to be concerned more with personal care than housing related support

- generates a great deal of paper and administrative work that can dissuade partners from getting involved and engaging with the programme

Health Act flexibilities

The Health Act 1999 gave health authorities and their local authority partners new powers to work together more effectively:

- **Pooled funds:** Partners can contribute agreed funds to a separate pot to spend on agreed projects for designated services.

- **Lead commissioning:** Partners can agree to delegate commissioning of a service to one lead organisation.

- **Integrated provision:** Partners can join together staff resources and structures to integrate service provision at all levels.

These flexible arrangements offer great potential to partners working together to achieve the Valuing People agenda.

Independence, Well-being and Choice Green Paper for Adult Social Care, 2005

In 2005 the government published a Green Paper which introduces a vision for adult social care in England for the next 10 to 15 years (www.dh.gov.uk). The key theme of this document is choice and control for people who receive services. One of the ways of achieving this is through individualised budgets which represent a development of the concept of direct payments and are intended to extend the range of people who are helped in this way to gain control of their lives. The government are, at the time of writing, running a series of pilots throughout the country which will inform the way individualised budgets will be developed. Consultation on the Green Paper is contributing to a Health and Social Care White Paper to be published at the end of 2005 or early 2006.

In Control

In Control is a partnership project that involves self-directed support (www.in-control.org.uk). A person with disabilities is enabled to have an individual budget and a decision-making process that is right for that particular individual. It is not just another form of direct payments but a scheme in which the money is actually allocated to the person who is then supported to design their own service. In Control may well prove to be the model that leads the way for individual budgets and empowerment of people with disabilities. In the words of Simon Duffey of In Control, 'The project wants to change the whole way social care is organised so that disabled people can be in control of their own support' (Community Care, 11 February 2005, in http://www.in-control.org.uk/downloads/20050301/Community_Care_Interview.pdf).

Local sources of funding

Now that I have looked at the main policies and guidance on a national level that influence the resources available for person centred planning I shall consider the different elements of funding that can be accessed on a local level, many deriving directly from this policy framework.

The benefits system

People with learning disabilities may be entitled to a range of different benefits depending on individual circumstances:

- Disability Living Allowance (DLA)

- Severe Disablement Allowance (SDA)

- Independent Living Fund (ILF)

These entitlements can contribute to the total package of money available for the person seeking to live independently, but finding your way through the minefield of regulations can be very difficult. When you completed Activity 20 you no doubt discovered that individuals may receive several different benefits, and each person may have a different package. All benefits derive from the Department of Work and Pensions (DWP) but some are administered locally, while others derive from a central location. Furthermore, some (such as the DLA support element) may be taken into account when an assessment of entitlement for funding is made by social services and so the final cost of the support package will be adjusted down.

Social services funded package

As explained above in the section on the NHS and Community Care Act, the local social services department has a responsibility to meet the assessed needs of disabled people. This responsibility may be discharged by arranging the purchase of services from other providers or by paying the money to the person as a direct payment for them to buy their own choice of services.

The local council will decide who is entitled to services by means of eligibility criteria, based on four bands of risk: critical, substantial, moderate and low (Leicester City Council, 2003). If the council has only enough resources to meet the assessed needs falling into some, but not all, of the bands its eligibility criteria will consist only of those bands that it can afford to meet. The same eligibility criteria must be applied to all client groups, which means that they cannot undertake to meet some needs for one group but not similar needs of another. This is called fair access to care services (FACS) (Department of Health, 2004). When someone has needs that are not eligible for community care services the council will guide them towards other council or community-based services which may be able to help.

As noted earlier, a weakness in this whole process is the domination of physiological and basic needs over social needs for friendships and relationships and combating loneliness. Unless person centred approaches are supported within care management, the wishes and aspirations expressed in a person centred plan will not necessarily be translated as a change in needs and so will not attract any additional funding. More resourceful ways to support implementation of plans therefore may be needed.

ACTIVITY 21: **Funding shortfalls**

Do you know how someone can apply for additional funding if there is a shortfall in the amount received in their benefits or from social services?

Find out all you can and write a brief account explaining:

● who would be responsible for addressing shortfalls in funding

● who the main contact would be in the funding authority

● what the process might be

Comment

You may be the person responsible for dealing with the shortfalls in funding or it may be a senior manager in your organisation. Often, a finance manager might take shortfalls in benefits forward, but ultimately they may need someone who knows about the person to complete a form explaining about their needs. Shortfalls in social services funding may be harder to address because often you are dealing with a care manager or team leader who does not make decisions about funding. Procedures will vary across the country, but there are a few main points to remember:

● Funding will only be increased if it can be proved that there has been a significant change in needs or that the original assessment was wrong.

● A reassessment will be required.

● Funding decisions will usually only be made at senior manager level (eg service manager or above).

● Social services departments have very limited resources and so a very clear case will need to be made if you are to have a chance of success.

● Person centred approaches will inevitably be hampered by limited resources that drive staff into task-focused responses, so be persistent.

Pooled budgets

As a result of the Health Act flexibilities, Partnership Boards can now form local agreements to pool budget and develop individualised services. For instance, the health authority and social services department may agree to pool their funding in order to streamline arrangements for enabling people to move out of a long-stay hospital into supported living.

Supporting people

Every social services department has its own Supporting People programme, which is funding the housing-related support of people who have moved into supported living. In 2004 each local authority was required to undertake extensive consultation in order to put forward proposals for a five-year development plan which will be used by the government to determine levels of future funding. The scheme has, it appears, been a victim of its own success, and future funding will concentrate on ensuring that services deliver value for money and that funds are targeted appropriately. In other words, Supporting People is costing the government too much and ways must be found to make it more cost-effective. There are likely, therefore, to be local cutbacks and it may become more difficult to access Supporting People funding for people with learning disabilities who are trying to achieve greater independence. 'Announcing a real terms 7% cut to the Supporting People budget over the next three years, officials from the Office of the Deputy Prime Minister said services for people with mental health problems or more severe learning difficulties were not appropriate for Supporting People funding' (Kumar, 2004).

Other sources of funding

Person centred planning does not necessarily cost more and may even cost less. However, it may frequently be found that a person seeking greater involvement in their community, participating as an equal citizen, cannot take the necessary steps forward without individualised support that they may not currently have access to. This will involve imaginative thinking, good communication and co-operation between all parties, a commitment to partnership working and the support of a key person (eg family member, person centred planning 'helper', keyworker, advocate or care manager). Some of the sources of support may be:

- an advocacy scheme that uses volunteers

- a charity committed to the needs of people with learning disabilities

- friends or family members

- local clubs, colleges and leisure centres that have the commitment to work with individuals

- funding from grant-making bodies

- volunteer workers

ACTIVITY 22: **Advocacy**

Find out as much as you can about advocacy schemes run in your locality and the ways in which they are supporting people with learning disabilities. Are they involved in delivering support to meet Valuing People objectives? Are they supporting people with person centred plans or representing people with learning disabilities on the local Partnership Board?

Comment

Advocacy schemes vary considerably across the country. For instance, in Leicester, Leicestershire and Rutland there are several schemes that provide advocacy support to people with learning disabilities, enabling people to speak out for themselves and to develop person centred plans. In particular, advocates have had an important role to play in helping people to move out of a long-stay hospital and make choices about their future lives.

Key points

- **Funding for person centred planning is influenced by several key pieces of legislation, government policy and guidance.**

- **Direct payments are an important route to empowerment and control.**

- **Partnership is needed to free up funding from different agencies.**

- **At a local level, funding may be complex and affected by local resource availability.**

- **Person centred planning relies on adequate funding, so shortfalls need to be addressed.**

Chapter 6

The impact of person centred planning

Introduction

This chapter differs from previous ones in that it is primarily reflective. It is crucial that managers are able to learn from the process of implementing person centred planning so that services can respond proactively to the impact that plans have on the lives of individuals and barriers can be overcome.

This chapter will help you to focus on:

- how to evaluate the impact of person centred planning

Evaluating the impact of person centred planning

Because this chapter is reflective it consists almost entirely of one activity. It is advisable, therefore, that you first take time to look back over all the reading and activity work you have covered so far and think about their relevance to your own work. When you have done this go on to Activity 23.

ACTIVITY 23: **Person centred planning: case studies**

This is a major activity and will give you the evidence to fulfil the assessment requirements for outcomes two, three and six of the LDAF Level 4 Unit Person Centred Planning which are covered in chapters 2, 5 and 6.

Write two case studies, each of about 1,000 words, describing and analysing the person centred planning process. The accounts should include:

- the process itself

- how the individual was supported
  (including the circle of support and workers in the service)

- the impact of the process

- the two-way relationship between resource allocation and the person centred plans

- how any barriers were removed

When you have completed the case studies compare and contrast the person centred process involved, drawing out key issues identified and reflecting upon any learning points.

Comment

Hopefully this exercise has helped to emphasise the very individual nature of every person centred plan. It may also have demonstrated the enormous impact that person centred planning has on the individual, on those around the person and on the way the service develops. Try to ensure that your account finishes with a clear reflection on this latter point and on how the process of evaluation has influenced the development of good practice in the service.

Add your finished account to the portfolio you are gathering to show that you have achieved the outcomes required for the LDAF Level 4 Unit 2 Person Centred Planning in a Learning Disability Service.

Key points

- **The process of developing a person centred plan is unique to each person.**

- **The process of person centred planning has a significant impact upon the person, all involved and the service.**

- **Evaluation of person centred planning is an important process to enable services to respond proactively to individual plans.**

Chapter 7

The wider context of person centred planning

Introduction

This chapter will draw together all the strands of this book and will help you to focus on:

- the wider context of services, both local and national, within which person centred planning takes place

Effects of person centred planning

Think back to what you have learnt about person centred planning in services. In chapter 4, I considered the barriers and challenges that might be faced when implementing person centred planning, but now I am going to reflect on the impact that person centred planning may have on services themselves. Sanderson et al (1997) give an example of change being encouraged through collaborative working between purchaser and provider, and stress the need for:

- both purchaser and provider to be involved together in implementing person centred plans

- commitment from the top downward

- a close link between care management and person centred planning

- a flexible approach to resource allocation to achieve desired outcomes

The issue about care management was discussed in chapter 5. It is vital for care managers to understand and be committed to person centred approaches so that care packages are designed around the person and services are supported to change. This means that both assessment and monitoring tools need to be redesigned so that they are person focused rather than service focused, and care managers need to receive training as facilitators of person centred planning.

For instance, in Leicester specific person centred planning training was developed for care management teams so that the training could focus on the assessment process and resource allocation to achieve the outcomes desired by person centred plans.

In this way care managers can be helped to develop contracts for services designed around the person, with staff allocation tailored to meet the person's needs. Monitoring can then be against the desired outcomes which are derived from the person centred plan and demonstrate that the things that are essential to the person are happening.

ACTIVITY 24: **Effects of person centred planning**

Consider what you have learnt so far and list the changes that person centred planning is likely to bring about for services:

- services for people with learning disabilities

- other community services, eg primary care services

Comment

I would imagine that the list of changes that you would anticipate for services for people with learning disabilities would include such things as greater flexibility, a move away from set working hours for staff, greater involvement of people with learning disabilities in decision-making and individualised packages rather than rigid group responses. What about the changes you might expect for other community services? I would have thought that the increased empowerment of people with learning disabilities would have a significant impact, driving workers to listen and take note of what people want. However, there are other implications with regard to health care that I shall now go on to consider.

Health action planning

Objective 6 of Valuing People is 'To enable people with learning disabilities to access a health service designed around individual needs, with fast and convenient care delivered to a consistently high standard, and with additional support where necessary' (Department of Health, 2001). Some key actions required to fulfil this objective are:

- reduction of health inequalities

- health facilitators to be identified for people with learning disabilities

- all people with a learning disability to be registered with a GP

- all people with a learning disability to have a health action plan

- development of specialist learning disability services, including services for people with challenging reputations

There are tremendous challenges here, but they are necessary if inequality is to be addressed and the standard of health care for people with learning disabilities is to be raised.

In 1998 Mencap carried out research around this subject and produced some worrying findings (Mencap, 1998). The research demonstrated that people with learning disabilities receive significantly inferior health services to other members of the community, despite documented evidence of health needs. For instance, although up to 63% of people with learning disabilities may have a visual impairment, 53% had not had a sight test in the previous two years despite the fact that 69% of these are over 40 years old and that statistics show that sight loss increases with age.

ACTIVITY 25: **Health**

Log on to the Internet and type in the following web address: www.mencap.org.uk/download/health_for_all.pdf

Read the research paper *The NHS - health for all?* and consider the difference that should be achieved once objective 6 of Valuing People is fully implemented. It will probably be helpful to go back to the White Paper *Valuing People* in order to remind yourself of the full discussion around health that is given here. This can be obtained from the Department of Health website.

Comment

It is very disappointing to reflect on the wide disparity in health provision that still exists between services for the general population and people with learning disabilities. Health action planning should be a useful mechanism for addressing this gap, but there is clearly a need to consider the relationship between health action plans and person centred planning. Person centred planning should encompass the whole of a person's life, not just parts of it, with different plans for different aspects such as health. It must be possible to draw up some principles around the interrelationship between health action plans and person centred planning, and I suggest that the following may be useful:

- The person needs an integrated approach to their life.

- A health action plan should be part of the person centred plan, not a separate document.

- Health facilitators need to co-operate closely with person centred planning facilitators.

There may be varying opinions about whether the health facilitator and person centred planning facilitator roles can be merged. Arguments in favour would suggest that if person centred planning facilitators incorporated health facilitation into their remit the danger of a shift towards the medical model approach would be avoided. However, the counter argument would be that the social model espoused by person centred planning facilitators would not necessarily provide a robust enough approach to identifying health needs and developing a plan (Thompson and Cobb, 2004).

Health action plans should gradually become a part of the planning process over the next few years with, it is hoped, a significant improvement in health care for people with learning disabilities. There is, however, an implication here for training and resource development with Primary Care Trusts (PCTs).

Quality services

Another aspect of Valuing People which interfaces closely with person centred planning is that of quality services. All local authorities are required to have a quality assurance framework that recognises and addresses the needs of people with learning disabilities (Department of Health, 2001). The requirement is for an integrated quality framework that applies across all agencies to ensure that the voices of people with learning disabilities are heard, that they are central to the process and that services are clearly accountable to them.

Many people are using the BILD quality network (www.bild.org.uk), which provides a framework of outcomes, developed by people with learning disabilities, their carers, supporters and professionals, to measure the quality of service provided. This focus on outcomes for people means that the quality framework is totally person centred in its approach. A commitment to person centred planning within a service should result in positive outcomes, which will be demonstrated by applying the quality framework as a monitoring tool.

Resources

The objectives of Valuing People are doubtless achievable, but there are cost implications. The government put in place a Learning Disability Development Fund of £50 million to be targeted on the key priorities of *Valuing People* (Department of Health, 2001). They also introduced an Implementation Support Fund of £2.3 million from 2001–04 which was to be used to fund advocacy, a new national information centre and helpline. These two funds were welcomed, but it must be acknowledged that for ongoing long-term progress, both locally and nationally, more is needed. A strong theme throughout is a requirement for partnership working (demonstrated, for instance, by the Health Act flexibilities that encourage pooled funds) but, unless there is a significant injection of funds at a national level, many people feel that Valuing People may run out of steam.

ACTIVITY 26: **Resource allocation**

Consider, in the light of this discussion, the impact that effective implementation of person centred planning may have on the allocation of resources at a national level (for instance, Supporting People, funding of social services, allocation of grants).

Comment

I believe that the main impact is going to be as a result of empowerment of people with learning disabilities to discover their voice and demand equal rights as citizens. There are many mountains to climb: Supporting People monies are being limited, the demands of children's services dominate local authority funding and the funds set up under Valuing People are time limited. But self-advocates are becoming more and more involved in decision-making at all levels and second class services are being rejected.

Key points

- **Person centred planning is resulting in empowerment of people with learning disabilities.**

- **As a result, services must change and become more responsive.**

- **Resource limitations may in future be challenged.**

- **Person centred planning and health action planning are intrinsically linked.**

- **Care management needs to take a person centred approach, with contracts being designed around the person.**

- **Quality can be monitored in a person centred way by using outcomes as standards.**

Conclusion

This book has addressed person centred planning which is the principle and system at the heart of learning disability services. You should now be able to:

- explore the principles, implementation and impact of person centred planning

- investigate ways of maximising the effectiveness of person centred planning for individuals

- review your own practice within the person centred planning process

- analyse the wider context in which person centred planning operates, including resources, constraints and opportunities

If you have worked through all the exercises you can now gather them into your portfolio to provide evidence of your knowledge and skills for this Level 4 unit of the Learning Disability Awards Framework. There is one more activity to undertake to complete this portfolio.

ACTIVITY 27: **Person centred planning: analysis**

Write about 1,000 words giving a critical analysis of:

- the distinctive nature of person centred planning

- its central place in current policy and practice

- reasons why person centred planning may be resisted or may be difficult to implement, and ways to address these

- the impact that person centred planning will have on the design and delivery of services if it is fully implemented

Add this analysis to your portfolio.

Comment

This last activity has summarised much of your learning which I hope will help to guide you in your future work with people with learning disabilities. Person centred planning depends upon input from each and every person involved and needs championing by committed and dedicated managers.

References

Atkinson, D., Jackson, M. and Walmsley, J. (eds) (1997) *Forgotten lives: exploring the history of learning disability* Kidderminster: British Institute of Learning Disabilities

BILD (2004) *More About Quality Network Services* Available from www.bild.org.uk (accessed 03.10.04)

Caldwell, P. *Making Progress* Videotape available from Concorde Films, Ipswich

Department of Health (2001) *Valuing People: A New Strategy for Learning Disability for the 21st Century* London: Department of Health

Department of Health (2003) *Direct Payment Guidance: Community Care, Services for Carers and Children's Services (Direct Payments) Guidance England 2003* Available from www.dh.gov.uk (accessed 29.09.04)

Department of Health (2005) *Independence, Well-being and Choice: Our Vision for the Future of Social Care for Adults in England* Available from www.dh.gov.uk (accessed 08.12.05)

Goffman, E. (1962) *Asylums* London: Penguin Books

Hughes, B. (1995) *Community Care and Older People* Birmingham: Open University Press,

Jerrom, C. (2004) 'Tell Us About Direct Payment Barriers' *Community Care* 7–13 Oct 2004

Kilbane, J. and Sanderson, H. (2004) 'What and How: Understanding professional involvement in person centred planning styles and approaches' *Learning Disability Practice* 7 (4) May 2004

Kinsella, P. (2000) *Barriers to Progress in Person Centred Planning* Birkenhead: Paradigm Available from www.paradigm-uk.org (accessed on 13.05.03)

Kumar, S. (2004) 'Funding' *Community Care* 2–8 Sept 2004

Leicester City Learning Disability Partnership Board. Person Centred Planning Working Group (2003). *Training Plan* Unpublished: Leicester City Council

Lyle O'Brien, C. and O'Brien, J. (2000) *The Origins of Person Centred Planning: A Community of Practice Perspective.* Decatur, Georgia: Responsive Systems Associates Available from www.paradigm-uk.org (accessed 03.05.03)

K100 Course Team (2004) *Care Systems and Structures* Milton Keynes: The Open University

Mencap (1998) *The NHS – Health for All?* Available from www.mencap.org.uk/download/health_for_all.pdf (accessed 29.09.04)

Neville, M. (1996) 'Around in a Circle' *Community Care* 29 Feb–6 March 1996

O'Brien, J. and Tyne, A. (1981) *The Principle of Normalisation: a Foundation for Effective Service* London: Values into Action

Office of Deputy Prime Minister (2004) *What is Supporting People?* London: OPDM

Routledge, M. and Gitsham, N. (2004) 'Putting Person Centred Planning in its Proper Place?' *Learning Disability Review* 9 (3) 21–26 Brighton: Pavilion

Sanderson, H., Kennedy, J., Ritchie, P. and Goodwin, G. (1997) *People, Plans and Possibilities: Exploring Person Centred Planning* Edinburgh: Scottish Human Services

Scottish Executive (2000) *Same as You? A Review of Services for People with Learning Disabilities.* Edinburgh: The Scottish Executive

Smull, M., Sanderson, H. and Burke Harrison, S. (1996) *Reviewing Essential Lifestyle Plans: Criteria for Best Plans* University of Maryland

Tizard Centre *Bringing People Back Home* Video series. Canterbury: University of Kent

Thompson, J. and Cobb. J. (2004) 'Person Centred Health Action Planning' *Learning Disability Practice* 7 (5) June 2004

Towell, C. (1980) *An Ordinary Life in Practice* London: The Kings Fund Centre

Walmsley, J. 'Social Care in the Community' K100 Course Team (1998) *Who Cares?* Milton Keynes: The Open University.

Wolfensberger, W. (1975) *The Origin and Nature of our Institutional Models* Syracuse, NY: Human Policy Press

Resources

Websites

Website addresses were correct at time of going to press

Association for Real Change (previously Association for Residential Care):
www.arcuk.org.uk

British Institute of Learning Disabilities:
www.bild.org.uk

Department of Health:
www.doh.gov.uk

In Control:
www.in-control.org.uk

Mencap:
www.mencap.org.uk

Paradigm:
www.paradigm-uk.org

People First:
www.peoplefirst.org.uk

Scottish Consortium for Learning Disability:
www.scld.co.uk

Scottish Executive:
www.scotland.gov.uk/ldsr

Michael Smull and Friends:
www.elpnet.net

Values into Action:
www.viauk.org

Valuing People Support Team:
www.valuingpeople.gov.uk

Useful publications

NB *In addition to the publications listed below, you will also find many of the books in the reference list useful.*

Duffey, S. (2004) *Keys to Citizenship* Birkenhead: Paradigm

Edge, J. (2001) *Who's in Control? Decision making by people with learning disabilities who have high support needs* London: Values into Action

Falvey, M., Forest, M., Pearpoint, J. and Rosenberg, R. (1997) *All my life's a circle using the tools: circles, maps & paths* Toronto, ONT: Inclusion Press

O'Brien, J. and Lyle O'Brien, C. (1998) *A Little Book about Person-Centred Planning* Toronto, ONT: Inclusion Press

People First, Manchester and Liverpool (1997) *Our Plan for Planning* Manchester: Manchester People First

Sanderson, H., Kennedy, K., Ritchie, P. and Goodwin, G. (1997) *People, Plans and Possibilities – exploring person centred planning* Edinburgh: SHS

Swindon People First and Norah Fry Research Centre (2002) *Journey to Independence: What self advocates tell us about direct payments* Kidderminster: British Institute of Learning Disabilities

Taylor, T. (2004) *Insistent Voices: stories on claiming identity* London: Kingston Advocacy Group